I'M EASY. . .

And I Have Bad Taste™

Angel Adams

First published by Dog Ear Publishing
4010 W. 86th Street, Ste H
Indianapolis, IN 46268
www.dogearpublishing.net

ISBN: 1-59858-187-2
Library of Congress Control Number: 2006930726

This book is printed on acid-free paper.

Printed in the United States of America

I'M EASY...
And I Have Bad
Taste!™

DISCLAIMER —
responsible sex.

Before we really get into how big of a slut I am or how stupid I can be, I do want to say that I am in no way condoning irresponsible sex. I have never had an STD, and I have never been pregnant. When I was younger I'm sure that had more to do with luck than anything else, but now as an adult I do my best to be responsible. I urge you to use condoms. Have consensual sex…no date raping, no coercion. Be responsible. Be safe. And if you're not safe and have happened to be lucky enough not to get a horrible disease and/or pregnant, remember, your luck won't last forever. It never does. So do what you need to do to be safe. USE CONDOMS. GET TESTED.

OK, that said, now on to the good stuff.

PREFACE

First of all, let me tell you what this book *isn't* about: advice. I'm not an expert, I'm just a girl who's been around the block a little—or a lot as the case may be. It's not about telling anyone how to date, love or have sex. I'm the last person to give anyone advice about anything…I'm giving you my opinion, and it's only my opinion. But any so-called "advice" to be had from these pages might be worth taking. That said, you just might want to do the exact opposite, since I'm still very single and have very bad taste. However, what you will find is that I see a lot of humor in my love life.

It's a manual *for me*, probably a little narcissistic, but whatever. I do suggest that any man who wants to date me (or women like me) read this…actually I like to think of it as "required reading" for all women in the gruesome dating world. If you "get" this book, you might begin to understand yourself and/or the stronger of the two sexes. Chicks of course.

Let's face it, everyone has had moments of easiness and/or bad taste. It's OK! (It's great actually.) Feel good about your decisions. Feel good about liking or wanting sex. More importantly, feel good about yourself—no matter what! And, if you identify with anything in these pages AND you are able to laugh at some of my easiness or bad taste, then mission accomplished. I have moved past any regret I may have had and moved on to unabashed narcissism and self-promotion!

If I offend, oh well…if I don't offend, you're my kind of person. If you're a hot guy who isn't abnormally weird, doesn't live with his mother, has an I.Q. in the triple digits, doesn't see violence as an option, isn't an addict of any kind *and* you think I might be your kind of girl, let my publicist know.

Enjoy! Or not. It's your life, but please try to make the best of it…and if that means reading this book with a sense of humor and taking it for what it is, pure observable life and sex from *my* point of view, then you're going to have a lot of fun.

Part I

1

I'M EASY

I'm twenty-nine years old. I'm attractive. I've got a good sense of humor. I'm intelligent. I'm caring. I have a pretty decent personality. I'm not a stalker. I'm not psycho. I'm a good cook. I'm a masseuse (a phenomenal one at that). I love wearing sexy lingerie. I like sex, A LOT. *And* I give an amazing blowjob, yet I still can't get a decent date.

People always ask me why I don't have a boyfriend. For years my typical response was, "Because I'm easy and I have bad taste!" I've found I'm not alone in my plight. My girlfriends and co-workers seem to have the same problem. We're all great girls, nothing too abnormally wrong with us. However, at times we all suffer from the same chick ailments: low self-esteem, unsubstantiated insecurities, Richter-scale PMS, attachment to complete morons or bad boys, and abnormal emotions that seem all too normal to us. We are guilty and are not too apologetic for these things. Sometimes I wish I could rid myself of many of my chick quirks and only keep the things that make me a woman, but what's the fun in that? I believe that the elements of being a woman—curves, soft skin, sensitivity, great-smelling hair, killer smiles, bedroom eyes, enjoyment of sex—make us attractive.

I love being a woman, but I am a chick. A cool chick, yes…but a chick nonetheless. And it's the chick in me that makes me nuts. Just like many other chicks out there. If anyone ever invents a cure for being a chick I might be the first to sign up…actually, I probably wouldn't because I just can't help liking being a cool chick. Not that it's helped me get a boyfriend, but it's helped in getting me laid…a lot.

I don't date, I just have sex. But I guess that's the world of dating in the twenty-first century. Unless you're one of those girls who are willing to settle right out of the gate, just to get married and be saddled with a couple of kids and a useless husband, then you must deal with dating. I, on the other hand, would rather be a spinster than have a useless husband. Thank God I'm allergic to cats, otherwise I'd be a spinster with a house full of them. And trust me, minus the house full of pussies, I'm on my way. And, the final paradox: I would never marry someone like me, so how can I ever expect someone *else* to want to marry me?

2

BAD TASTE

What is bad taste, really? Dating a married man? A man with bad hygiene? No money? No car? No class? A criminal background? Whatever it is exactly, my bad taste may be someone else's bounty. In turn, my ideal is probably someone else's bad taste. To each her own…I just happen to believe my bad taste is phenomenally BAD. And I'm not alone in my belief. My brand of bad taste is an epidemic according to my peers.

If the old saying, "You can't help who you fall in love with," is true (and I think it is), then I'm SCREWED! But then, how can you have a choice in who you lust after, if you don't have a choice in who you fall in love with? And lusting is all I'm really guilty of. However, it's gotten way out of control, and I'm beginning to wonder if I am predestined to lust after the wrong people. Which only means who knows who I'll fall in love with.

Admit it. There are plenty of you out there like me who have this serious "mental condition." I think we should form a support group—a place where we could get together, compare stories, and then cry on each other's shoulders. I'm guessing I would stand out even within that group because not only do I have bad taste, but I also have extremely bad judgment.

Bad taste is kind of hard to explain. In the moment, I never think the target of my affection is a total loser or a jerk…well, that's not always true...but mostly I don't realize what I'm getting myself into until it's too late. It's like I've stumbled into a really deep, dark pit of stupidity and lust and just can't find my way out. That's why we need a Bad Dater's Anonymous support group; and maybe a 24-hour hotline we could call just in time to talk us away from the jerk or asshole of the moment.

I think bad judgment is a little easier to explain, let me illustrate. I have knowingly dated a man who had a girlfriend; had sex with a man who is married; fallen in love (or lust) with a man I work with; fucked a man who would never want to see me outside the bedroom, or broom closet or wherever; dated a man who was completely and obviously commitment phobic; gave a married man a blowjob because it was easier than saying no and risking my job; the list could go on and on.

Now, for any of you judging me by my own bad judgment, save me the lecture on what comes around goes around, *karma*, and all that other moral crap. Clearly, I've never claimed to be righteously moral or to have good taste or judgment. I also know there probably will be someone like me out there who will fuck my husband or boyfriend. I would deserve it, and I fully expect the man I end up with to cheat on me. I probably would if I had to date or marry *me*.

I'm not saying I *want* the man I'm with to cheat on me. I sure hope he doesn't! The hopeless romantic in me wants to believe that if ever a good man finds me and makes me his, he would not have the desire to cheat...but, not too many good, non-cheating men have made their way into my path. In the meantime, I won't be surprised when he cheats. BUT, I will be pleased if he doesn't whore around with the first chick like me who crosses his path. I figure it this way, I'm confessing my bad judgment and deeds right now for all to see, and I can now move forward to make more bad judgment decisions in the future with a clear conscious.

But let's be honest: All of these lapses in judgment can be easily explained away by my own inability to commit. It's my defense mechanism for my inability to be truly intimate or commit to a real relationship. I use sex as my only weapon of defense, keeping at bay all those who might hinder my lonely single-hood, and it's a weapon I use well and often. Committing to good and frequent sex is the only thing I'm not afraid of committing to.

I do want a relationship, but I don't. I'm a full-fledged commitment phobe, but at the same time I would like a healthy, happy relationship…I just don't want to take the risk. You might have heard this before, but I run for the hills if *getting hurt* might be an option. This is a recent discovery for me that kind of explains some of my past bad taste/bad judgment. I guess that's why I'm attracted to men who are completely unavailable—emotionally and for a relationship. That way, when the so-called relationship unravels, it's not my fault. *He's* the loser. *He's* the one who has the problem. *He's* the one who doesn't want a relationship. It's *his* fault, not mine, and that's all that matters to me. I'm guilt free. When it all comes down, I'm a normal woman who wants a relationship that works…end of story!

Unfortunately, I don't escape these moments of bad judgment without some sort of emotional harm. Even though I repeat the same bad choices over and over, I can't seem to learn how to not get hurt. I pretty much feel it's my fault on some level. Like most women, I'll think, "I'm not good enough," or "I must have done something wrong." But of course, I did do something wrong, I got involved with an *idiot*. Oh wait a minute…I am the IDIOT, so it must be my fault. (If you're a guy, I dare you to try and logically piece *that* together.)

Anyway, I do believe my horniness is responsible for my downfall. Even if I were capable of making a good decision, eventually my sex drive would get in the way and literally screw it up. Sometimes I end up sleeping with a man I don't want to get involved with. We hang out, have sex, get closer, but the "relationship" is doomed to begin with because I don't want a relationship, I just want sex. It's similar to a guy getting cuter the more you get to know him. I hate that. Because you wake up one day and realize the hunk-of-burning-hot-man-body you thought you were laying next to for months on end is really a Frankenstein-like troll. They just grow on you like mold before your very eyes, and you don't even know it's there until it's too late. You can't get rid of those cooties fast enough!

Don't get me wrong, I can get totally into a guy who's only redeemable feature is his personality. Anyone who knows me knows that I've dated some completely hideous-looking men. I think I do it because I would hope that, at times, people fall for my personality too. I would much rather "he" fall for "me," not my vagina!

In the end, my friends tell me it's not my fault that I keep attracting the type of guys that I do. Because it's not really a conscious decision, or is it? There seems to be some underlying force in me that loves the chaos. Jack, one of my best male friends, once said to me, "It's so wonderful that you don't do it on purpose," that I give the major losers in my life a chance and also begin to care about them, knowing full well that it will never work out.

I'm convinced it's the chaos of my love life that keeps me going…better yet, the chaos of my hot and heavy, orgasmic sex life keeps me going. At least my exploits serve to entertain my friends to some degree, and to me that's even more important than some guy.

Let's get this straight. I'm not asking you to feel sorry for me or pity me. I realize I have issues, but I have come to terms with a lot of them. I am aware of my behavior; I even understand my behavior. But I am not choosing to alter it yet—or *ever* for that matter. I do think that you get back what you put out there in the world, and it's obvious to me that I'm putting out some really fucked-up vibes to get back what I'm getting. Maybe the problem is I'm just "putting out" too much to begin with?

I do hope that someday a man who is worthy will find and rescue me. But I know if I do the picking and choosing, I'll end up with yet another horribly bad choice, I'm sure. How do other women do it? Should I go hang out in posh hotels, waiting for a successful businessman to sweep me off my feet? Pretend to be someone I'm not and trick the wrong guy into loving me? Go to single millionaire "mixers" in hopes the man of my dreams will pick me out of the crowd of bimbos? I figure that's not really letting a man *find* me if I plant myself somewhere to "accidentally" meet him at the right place and the right time, huh? But still, I would like the right guy to find me…find me irresistible, sexy, and perfect. Is that too much to ask?

3

THE FACT IS

*O*scar Wilde wrote, "…a woman who tells you her age will tell you anything."

I have found that I lack a verbal edit button in my everyday life, meaning I have a tendency to say whatever's on my mind, most of the time. Excluding, I hope, hurtful and completely unimportant information. But I think that's a good thing. People who keep things secret will only make themselves sick and miserable. I used to be like that, and it really did make me sick. I just kept everything in until I wanted to explode. Now I try and let everything out whenever possible, and it's working for me, so far at least.

Well, I've already told you I'm 29 years old and not getting any younger. So you'll have to trust me when I tell you I'm pretty much an open book. I won't tell you everything. Some things must be left to the imagination. The names have been changed to protect the not-so-innocent. Some situations and facts have been altered…mostly so my friends, family, and ex-boyfriends can't figure out who exactly it is that I've slept with. I won't disclose numbers either, but you may be able to guess the ballpark, whether it's a little league field or Wrigley Field is up to interpretation. Anything else you want to know I'm sure I'll tell you…even if you don't want to know, I'm sure I'll tell you.

I'm not saying I never lie. If it saves my ass or someone's feelings I am not opposed to an occasional fib. I just generally try not to do it. I think lying can be a form of manipulation and I go out of my way not to manipulate. Then again, now that I think about it, maybe not manipulating is its own form of manipulation. Hmmmm. That's something for me to ponder. I know manipulating is sometimes the only advantage women have, maybe that's why I'm still single.

Actually, to be absolutely honest, the full and accurate quote by Oscar Wilde is not quite as I said. The exact quote is as follows:

> "One should never trust a woman who tells one her real age. A woman who would tell one that would tell one anything."

So, I guess I'm not so honest after all...or I'm so honest that I shouldn't be trusted, that's the likely scenario. Either way my conscience is clean. I will tell you that when I began writing this book I told my friends, lovers, and family that "anything they say or do can and will be used FOR or against them at anytime," especially if it's half way funny, sexual, or entertaining. They've all had fair warning. I certify that the following is a fairly accurate and hopefully entertaining account, whether you believe it or not. And sometimes I don't believe it myself, and I *lived* it.

4

MY PSYCHOSIS

My psychosis runs deep and long and is accompanied by years of therapy and self-discovery. I haven't found out much through these years of soul searching, but I know one thing, I'm far from done with therapy. I've also learned, we are all a little crazy…I'm just willing to admit it. Sadly, admitting you have a problem isn't half the battle…it's just the beginning. That is true in so many areas of my life.

The good news (for the men anyway) is that I no longer use the man I'm with as a psychotic sounding board. I pay good money to lessen the torture I make the men in my life endure. Doesn't sound fair for my poor psychiatrist, does it?

I know I'm a nut job, but what woman isn't? However, I'm not a psycho in the traditional jilted ex-girlfriend kind of way. If you don't want me, that's fine. I know all of the losers I date CANNOT get much better than me. They may like the next one more, but it doesn't mean she's better.

You see, that's the beauty of bad taste, I'll always be the best they've ever had…with few exceptions of course, mostly because there are lots of other chicks out there with bad taste too. I can sleep at night knowing I'm right about this. I know the chance of seeing my loser ex with an amazing person who has no noticeable flaws is minimal.

That said, there is nothing worse than being upgraded. It's the biggest slap in the face you can get, especially when you have bad taste to begin with. Generally, the few times I've actually seen my exes out, they've always been with someone older, uglier, and/or more tainted...either that or I'm too drunk to care. Lucky for me my most recent ex ended up knocking up an ugly crack whore (literally). I've got my freedom and he's got NOTHING worth bragging about except another kid he can't afford.

I know that my exes probably care and love the next one more, but at least I'll have primed them for a real relationship. Almost every guy I dated in high school, and even some in college, married the next person they dated after me. I must be doing something right, either that or I'm scaring the hell out of the guy from dating anymore. I should get a reverse wedding present from the happy couple, you know sort of a "thank you" for not being good enough or for being the nut job that I am. Is that wrong? I could really use a new toaster oven or a new set of silverware. They could even re-gift one of their unwanted wedding presents, I wouldn't mind...as long as it's not monogrammed. Beggars can't be choosers, and I don't beg much, unless that turns you on.

Even though I'm against prostitution for me, I am thinking I ought to start taking donations from the men in my life to go toward my therapy. I spend half my sessions on men, sex, men, relationships, men, my bad taste, men, sex, and men. It's only fair to make those who helped create the psychosis donate to the cause. They are being spared my driving by their homes six or seven times a night right? Just think, therapy may be the only thing stopping me from really going over the edge and becoming that "Fatal Attraction" bitch that every man fears. If it wasn't for therapy, if you just give me the chance and you push the wrong buttons, I could boil your bunny.

Seriously, I surprise myself at times. What goes on inside my head even scares me and I'm used to *the voices*. I can't imagine what a man would think, or even my doctor for that matter, if they could actually hear what goes on inside my brain. The mind of a woman is a scary, incomprehensible thing and men should feel lucky that they don't, or can't, read our minds—if they could, they all would probably become celibate, or gay.

5

FAMILY TREE

*I*f it isn't obvious by now…I'm a Ho, and I'm proud of it. It's a fact of my life; I can't deny it and TRUST ME I've tried. My mother is a Ho. And she would never say differently. Just ask her. Then again, her maiden name is Ho, so she didn't have much of a choice in the matter. I guess all these years I've just been trying to live up to the family name. It is a piece of my lineage, part of my heritage. No one can ever hold it against me or fault me for living up to standards set forth before I was born.

I grew up in a very small farm town in Washington state where, like many other places, there wasn't much to do except drugs, drinking and sex. I never did drugs, but I drank a lot and had even more sex. For the longest time I thought I was the biggest slut ever to walk the streets, not literally of course. I know I was having a lot more sex than the other girls I grew up with, but hey, I was probably having a lot more fun than them too. I'm still probably having a lot more fun…thank God.

There's a big difference between being easy and being a total whore. I think I'm just the average person's "easy," not a *complete* whore. Webster's definition of 'whore' is "someone who is sexually promiscuous." Okay, that would mean me, *and* everyone else out there having pre-marital sex—but by societal standards I'm probably not as much of a slut or whore as you might think.

There are many of my peers who have slept with many more men than me. I do not consider them whores, and even if they were, so what, I don't care. Otherwise we would have nothing better to talk about than our stupid jobs. Instead we get to discuss the juicy details of length, size, girth and technique. There's nothing better than sex gossip after a hard days work…and there's nothing that women would rather talk about than how many times a guy can go in a night, and how many times he was actually successful in getting us off.

Most of my male friends have slept with a phenomenal amount of women, and they are very proud of it. I pale in comparison, but I really am trying. However, it seems that no matter how hard I try I can't seem to match the numbers or the stamina of my male counterparts.

The numbers are even higher with the gay men in my life. They have more one-night stands and group sex than almost any heterosexual I know. I don't mean to sound like I'm judging, because I'm jealous their numbers are extraordinary high compared to my paltry digits. When my friend Robert comes home from a gay bar empty handed it's not unusual for him to pick a guy up off the street or log onto a chat room to meet up for some middle of the night lovin'. Now that takes balls.

Robert makes me look like a nun. I mean, I don't want you to misinterpret my being easy for giving it up to just anyone. Sure, if I am attracted to you, or I like you, or even tolerate you, and you, in turn, make some sort of effort, the odds are I would lie down like a cheap whore for you. But I won't just lie down for anyone…if you assume I'll have sex with you and act accordingly arrogant, you might as well go home and have at it with yourself, a bottle of Jergens, and a *Hustler*.

6

DOMESTICATED GODDESS

*M*aybe I'm easy because I am flawed to perfection…I'm a walking contradiction. Really I am, at least in the "house wife" department…something I wish I wasn't good at. But I have been bred and raised to wait hand and foot on my man of the moment whether I want to or not. I have no free will in the matter; it doesn't matter because my genetic make-up has destined me to a life of servitude. My mother, being Asian and all, has drilled into my head that the only way into a man's heart, and to keep his affection, is to cook for him, clean for him, and bend over for him (literally and figuratively)…basically, be at his beck and call, every request, every demand, to do as I'm told. My Hell hath come to fruition…God only knows I can't help it.

I had been dating a guy, Barry, for only a couple of months when his uncle came into town for a visit. While he was here, he informed me that I cooked some of the best meals he'd ever tasted. I cleaned up after both of them and looked sexy as hell in the process. After about two or three days of my service and attention, out of the blue, Barry's uncle said, "You don't look like the domesticated type!" He is SO right, and I know it was meant as a compliment but it wasn't…at least not to me! I dream the little dream of being the modern woman who can't cook, hires a housekeeper, has a headache to avoid BAD sex, and who is completely void of needing a man. Unfortunately, I like having a man around, I love sex, I can cook really well, and I clean and do laundry like the best of them. I'm goddamn Martha Stewart…only young, sexy and broke!

When I say my mother is full Asian, I mean full-out Asian…in every way. Anyone who knows an Asian woman raised in her native land understands what I'm talking about. At one point in my mother's life she was the stereotypical subservient Asian, the kind that waited on her man hand and foot and gave him sex whenever he wanted it, whether she was in the mood or not. Well, in that one area, like mother like daughter. But I don't want to be my mother…at least my mother of twenty years ago.

In the last twenty years, she has been fully Americanized. She's as materialistic and demanding as the average American woman, but to her credit, she still knows how to take care of her man. She wakes up to make her husband breakfast even though he leaves for work hours before she does. She cleans for him and takes care of him in every way and feels that it's her wifely duty to stay fit and trim and still wear lingerie…it's definitely a lost art, but I guess I'm glad I've learned some of its value.

It's really weird. I'm more domesticated and capable of being domesticated than any of my other friends who want the marriage-baby trap at all costs. Yet I do not want that life for myself. I do not want to live that life…the life of a working housewife, cooking and cleaning and holding a full time job and raising some guy's kids. Unfortunately, my mother created a control freak, a hygiene-clean freak, and, well, a plain old freak just by giving birth to me. Half the time when I'm dating a guy I feel more like his maid than his girlfriend…not because he makes me feel like that, but more because I date complete slobs and I can't help but clean up after him for fear of getting SARS, a Staph infection or something much worse just from using his shower.

I like my environment to be clean, so if it's dirty I clean it; I don't wait for a guy to do it, even if it's his place. I don't like eating out all of the time, I enjoy cooking and I'm good at it, but if a man *expects* me to cook he might as well order out; I do it because I want to. It's amazing how some people expect things after you start to do them voluntarily. I can't imagine how bad it would be for me if I couldn't do the things I can…not only would I still not be able to keep a man, I wouldn't be able to get past a one night stand. I can't imagine living like a pig, not being able to boil water and not enjoying sex as much as I do. However, if I couldn't do these things maybe, just maybe, I would end up with a man who didn't *want* me to do those things. He would hire a staff for me, and let me just look pretty and shop all day. If only!!

I am always in fear of being too self-sufficient and too independent for the average man's taste. They go running for the hills after they find out I really don't need them for anything but a shoulder to cry on (don't forget my emotional neediness), a little cuddling and sex…men just love all that. It's probably the exact reason why I have so many men knocking down my door and fighting over my attentions…sarcasm intended.

My domestication even has gone so far as to be handy around the house…too handy, probably, but I can't help it. I can fix a squeaky door, leaky faucet, stopped drain, and more. Better than the average man…if something's broke I'll fix it, I'm not going to wait around for weeks listening to it drip, especially after I've asked my man who hasn't gotten around to it. I'm too independent I know, but if you're not going to do it in a timely fashion, get out of my way. I was a tomboy and hung out with my father and brothers a lot, I worked on a farm and know my way around.

Once when I was helping one of my girlfriends move she broke, or jammed, the moving truck hydraulic—the hydraulic is the mechanism that allows the bed of the truck to move up and down. She and all of her other friends panicked, including the men. She didn't want to return a broken truck and lose the $300 deposit. The men attempted to fix it by kicking it and hitting it with a hammer, while I watched calmly off to the side. Finally, I asked for a butter knife (that's the only tool I needed), I crawled underneath the truck with my faithful tool and worked my magic while her Gucci'ed friends looked on, dumbstruck. Moments later, I emerged, dirty and greasy but, successful. The hydraulic was fixed, the women altogether impressed and the men emasculated, and I am now a dinner party story to all of her other friends. I am—and always will be—the "girl who fixed a truck with a butter knife." I've always wanted to be infamous, but that isn't exactly what I had in mind.

I definitely like to feel needed, but the fastest way for me to feel bitter is to be with a man who *expects* everything. There's nothing worse than being taken for granted when you're scrubbing someone else's floors. It's happened too often to me, so I'm learning, slowly but surely, not to be the domesticated goddess my family has bred so well—and comes so naturally to me. I do not want to be your maid or your house bitch, just your sex slave. At least until I meet the next man who loves great homemade lasagna, a clean pressed shirt, and rocks my world in bed like no other!

Part II

7

PRUDE SNOB

I am a prude snob…that means I don't like prudes much. I'm not saying I don't like them as people…I just don't like what they stand for. Prudish behavior? Prudes? I don't understand them; they don't put out and typically judge the girls who do. If you've slept with less than 10 men in your life, the odds are we won't get along. And if we do get along, I'm sure I'd spend most of the time just trying to get you laid—or trying to get me laid by one of your cute guy friends that you're too prudish to sleep with. Someone should be getting sex, and if it's not you it might as well be <u>me</u>.

I do have a few friends who, in my eyes, are total PRUDES, but we're friends nonetheless. They often tell the easy ones in their life (me) that you "should wait and get to know a guy first…be friends before you have sex with them." If I hear that one more time I'm going to puke. Seriously, I don't tell them over and over to fuck the guy they happen to like or have a crush on before they get to know the name of their man's first pet or what his favorite toy was as a kid. So, why should I be on the receiving end of numerous lectures on abstinence and/or waiting?

Recently, Gina, one of my prude friends said: "I'm not as sweet as you think; I can be bad, you know." For one, that put some scary-ass mental pictures in my head and two, that could be true. But really, how much time would a man have to put in to reach that "bad" girl? Months? Years? I'm sure she is "bad". With six months to a year or more between partners, she's got to have a lot of pent-up sexual energy just waiting to bust at the seams. Gina is probably just a dirty girl at heart…crazy in bed; a dominatrix, just waiting for the right victim, I mean boyfriend, to control and torture. I do hope all of the above is true because it's much better than being a boring prude.

This is the same person who was kind of dating a guy for a month or so and mentioned that she wanted to do something "special" for her man. I said she should give him an old fashioned blowjob. All Gina could do was blush. She thought I was teasing, but really what better present to a man who's probably got a serious case of blue-balls from dating her for the last month? That's what I'd get a man I was attracted to if I thought he had a bunch of pent up sexual energy that was just dying to be released.

I also have a few married friends who were prudes before their married days. The funny thing with them is that they love my easy, slutty sto-ries…living vicariously through my conquests. If they weren't married they might only be having sex just once in awhile, but since they're married and, hopefully, having regular sex, they can't really judge me for wanting my own regular sex; even if I want regular sex with not-so-regular men.

I honestly don't know how to date a guy and not sleep with him within the first three dates, OK the first date, generally, if I like him…well, unless he's a gentleman and doesn't put the moves on. It's just not me to stop the urges, and if it feels good I do it. I did wait once for an entire month before I slept with a guy, but it was only because I made a bet with my friends. First, my friends bet I couldn't wait six dates, which would generally be insane, but I wasn't sure I was attracted to Steven so I made that deadline with ease. So much ease that they challenged me again. They wanted me to wait for a month. At that point I kind of wanted to prove to myself that I could do it, even though there was nothing in it for me, no sex (obviously), no money, no dinner, no nothing. It was really silly and pointless because we were having oral sex until our mouths hurt—more than I had since high school. When Steven and I finally did have sex, it didn't mean any more to me than if we would have fucked on the first night. Unfortunately, it meant something to him because he'd never waited either, which is prob-ably why he fell in love with me.

Not to mention that waiting didn't help me get to know him. Steven ended up being an alcoholic and a coke junkie, two things I didn't find out about until *weeks* after I'd slept with him. However, I must say, Steven was fabulous in bed; he's still on my top ten list for best overall lovers. He wanted it anytime and any place. But I digress. Waiting made no difference except prolonging the inevitable GREAT and frequent SEX, something I will never delay again.

If I actually waited to get to know a guy really well before I had sex with him, I'd probably never sleep with any of them. Especially since most of the men I get involved with (i.e. have sex with), I wouldn't really want to get INVOLVED with in the first place. I generally know from the beginning that a relationship isn't in the cards, and if I got to know these guys very well, I would no longer want to have sex with them. So what's the point of waiting, right? At least in my case, most of the men I attract, or am attracted to, wouldn't wait around for the sex for very long anyway.

Why are prudes prudes I wonder? I know a few who are prudes because they've never had an orgasm. Now that's a horrible phenomenon, I can't even imagine the torture. Recently, I discussed this with one such prude, and surprisingly Theresa said she'd be more apt to have meaningless sex if she enjoyed it. Until then I didn't know if she realized what she was missing, but she won't REALLY know what she's missing until she has that all too illusive orgasm. I know that if I'd never had an orgasm, which I would rather die than live that fate, I guess I wouldn't see the point of sex either. Even though sex in general, even without an orgasm, is a highly enjoyable activity.

Either that, or more than likely, I'd try to sleep with as many men as possible until one of them got it right. Better yet, I'd invest in some good porn, some sex toys and just do it myself until I figured it out. Orgasms are good, very good…everyone should have them! You should never have to rely on a man for anything, even an orgasm because there are always options. Use a man when you *want* a man! And be able to do it yourself when you want, which is even more important.

It really is a sad thing when I hear about the lack of orgasms from my friends and colleagues. Another orgasm-less friend of mine in college, Josie, didn't have one until some of us girls got her a vibrator for her birthday and told her to go at it alone until she figured out what if felt like to have a leg shaking orgasm <u>and</u> how to do it right. How can a man give a girl an orgasm if she can't give one to herself? Josie was 22 years old at the time; a handful of wasted years…how sad is that? She was successful finally, and it completely changed her life. Josie went from barely tolerating sex to actually looking forward to it. Imagine that, loving the act of sex, being able to achieve an orgasm, and knowing that it's all worthwhile. Amazing!

I have a female relative who went through one entire marriage without ever having an orgasm. She's been fixed up good since, but I think that would have been grounds enough for divorce, even if her husband hadn't hit on me. Which, for the record, I didn't even kiss the jerk-stuttering-troll, even though she still thinks I slept with him. Even I don't have *that* bad of taste. I've been completely emotionally damaged by the fact that anyone I know would think I would sleep with him. Did I say YUCK?!

Sorry, personal messages aside, a percentage of the proceeds of this book should go to an educational program teaching young women how to have an orgasm. Not that I have one every time I have sex, but now that I'm a little older and wiser its definitely more frequent, and I absolutely know how to give myself one, too. Stress and the man definitely play a role in achieving the perfect orgasm, but practice makes perfect as they say, and believe me, I'm trying to be perfect.

8

SUV SIZE SEX DRIVE

I am horny! Hear me roar!

I love sex, and I've got the sex drive of an 18-year-old boy. But instead of it slowing down, it's only the beginning. How scary is that? I can't imagine wanting sex more than I already do. If I go a month without sex, I really miss it. It makes me nuts to the point where I avoid the produce section of my supermarket because the shape of certain vegetables makes me too horny. If I go a couple of days, I crave it more than anything. I know it's a sexual and emotional need, sometimes one more than the other, but nonetheless I miss it and want it and need it bad.

Since high school, the longest I've ever gone without sex is about six months, and it nearly killed me. I think I was depressed at the time, so I didn't notice it at first. I'm sure it didn't bother me as much as it normally would, even though it was six months without <u>any</u> sexual contact. I think that may have even included masturbation too. Ironically, during most of this time I was involved in a serious relationship with a live-in boyfriend.

I'm a bigger slut than most of my male friends, but I enjoy making them feel easier than I am. I don't let men get away with that stupid double standard. Women can enjoy sex just as much as men. We also can want and crave variety at times, just like a guy. I admit that I get attached, but I can have meaningless sex too. I'm not ashamed to admit to my desires and sexual needs. I'm only human…a horny human, but human nonetheless.

I think I've always been like this, over sexed that is! In high school during the summer I worked as a truck driver for one of the local farms. I would wait in the field with my truck for it to get loaded with grain, and then I'd take it to the storage facility. The days were very long, from dawn to dusk, and *very* boring. We worked seven days a week until the season was over, so I never got to see my boyfriend, Alex, who was younger than me and didn't work.

Alex sometimes would come out to visit me in the fields. It would make the day go by quicker. It didn't hurt that whenever the opportunity arose, we'd start fooling around in the truck. We knew that was the only real reason for those visits. I would have him come out and visit me a couple of times a week. We would have good, hot, sweaty, dirty sex…just what a horny teenager needs. The danger and excitement of getting caught didn't hurt the situation either. I miss those non-stop carefree sex days. Oh, to be young again, and not pushing thirty!

That summer he got caught shoplifting condoms. (We were going through them faster than I could get them from the free clinic.) It was totally embarrassing for me since I was the older woman and corrupting him with my sexual ways, but he was wearing his arrest like a badge of honor. I don't think his parents liked me much after that. He was a virgin before me. I can say it was probably the last time a guy kept up with my unusually high sex drive. How sad is that? That was almost fifteen years ago, and I've since been forced to curb my desire and settle for the less-than-sexual declining drive of the men I'm around. I have a feeling I'm going to be a sugar momma or a cradle robber in my old age. Call me Mrs. Robinson. Otherwise, I'll have to settle on sex once a week at most, and who wants that?

It seems that in American society, maybe all societies, women are only supposed to want sex from one partner at a time. We are expected to be happy with the same man every time. When, in reality, the older we get the better sex gets, the more we are in touch with our sexuality, and the more we want it. How is one man who is getting older, with a decreasing sex drive, supposed to keep us satisfied? I don't think it's possible; maybe that's why more and more women are cheating on their men?

I just don't understand why sex can't be just sex, and love can't be just love. Keep the meaningful sex where it belongs…in romance novels. It doesn't mean that meaningless sex can't be enjoyable…quite the contrary. Sometimes, when emotions are out of the way, one can focus on the pleasures of the moment. Meaningful sex, now and then, is a hindrance to just having a lot of fun.

I'm not knocking meaningful sex…I just haven't had a lot of *good* meaningful sex. The meaningful relationships I've been in have produced not so great sex. It doesn't mean I cared for them any less, but sex is too important in a relationship for it to not meet everyone's needs.

Whenever I'm bored, all I think about is sex…call it a hobby. I'll be in the grocery store and check out every man in the place…wondering about his penis size, whether he's good in bed, does he think I'm attractive, would he want to have sex with me, etc. It's non-stop. At times I wonder if there's something wrong with me; then I realize that everybody thinks about sex to some degree, it's just they don't seem to talk about it much or admit to it. I find talking about sex highly enjoyable…a very good way I can think of to pass the time.

Like I said, I'm always looking for it even if I'm not involved with someone, sometimes when I am, so I don't really understand self-imposed abstinence. A friend of mine, Sarah, who was once a prude but has since had a couple of flings—I'm very proud, decided she was going to abstain from sex for at least six months. I thought it was kind of funny since at the time she was not having a lot of sex to begin with. She said she was looking for "sex that wasn't tawdry." What's wrong with tawdry? I like cheap tawdry sex, that's at least half of the sex I've had…okay, that's most of the sex I've had.

The entire abstinence endeavor is just odd to me. How can any warm-blooded young woman voluntarily choose to not have sex? Sarah said the men stuff was just kind of getting in the way…clouding her judgment and taking up a lot of time. Fortunately, the pledge did not last long and her sexual career began again.

I think I get turned down for sex more than the average 17-year-old guy, especially since I date the "older man." It's really a blow to my ego, but I really can't take it personally since I *always* want it. So far, I don't know any man who can keep up with me. I guess I've got to *expect* to get turned down considering how often I want it. A 33-year-old man I dated for a while was always turning me down, which I didn't understand because, when we did have it, we had GREAT sex. He told me that I drained him and that I was trying to kill him with sex. I told him that maybe I was, and that it would have been much easier than breaking up with him. The first night we had sex we did it three or four times in 12 hours. He created a good and healthy expectation of our future sex life; an expectation he didn't live up to. He did say that he didn't mind if I had sex with other men, as long as it was in front of him, and it wasn't emotional. I don't think I like the idea of being involved with a man who is willing to share me, but it's good to know that it's an option.

More men than I can count have called me a nymphomaniac. There's nothing wrong with that, is there? When I'm in a relationship. I expect sex. A lot. Why *else* would you be in a relationship? Why deal with the heartache? For regular sex of course. For really good, regular sex. I say it proud, I say it loud...I LOVE SEX, A LOT! So, give it to me next time I ask, will you?

9

ADVICE FROM THE TRENCHES

*I*f you think I give bad advice, wait until you hear some of the advice I've received from all sorts: the women in my life, books, magazines, movies, and men. Thankfully, I don't listen very well. But then again, I am still single with very bad taste. Maybe I should consider following some of the advice I have received from all of those *experienced* women, most of whom have been married at least once. Nah…I'd rather do it my way. The hard way!

For one, those dating advice and explanation books on "men" are such a waste—not that I've read them all, but I've glanced at a few. Almost every girl I know has *Men are from Mars, Women are from Venus*. I've heard it's very insightful in understanding how men think and crap like that, but come on, I'd rather experience it first hand than read about it in a book. Every man is different, just as there is no book out there that explains women accurately.

I think the worst of them all is *The Rules*, written by Ellen Fein and Sherrie Schneider. For those not familiar with this book, it's all about following "rules" to get a man to commit to you. Specifically, how to *manipulate* a man into falling in love with you. How to *not* be yourself and have a man fall in love with the fake you. It's probably the worst book I ever skimmed. Like women don't have a bad enough reputation for being gold diggers, liars, psychos, manipulators, etc. I'm ashamed to say that I actually own this book...I bought it as "research". Here's some of the unbelievable advice it gives:

Rule #2 Don't talk to a man first...

Are we in the Stone Age? Are we incapable of initiating conversation? There's nothing wrong in letting a guy know you're interested, especially with all of the insecure men out there. They need a little bit of encouragement. I'm not saying send them a box of condoms, just a simple, "Hello, how are you doing?" No commitment, just an opening.

Rule #5 Don't call him and rarely return his calls...

If you want to talk to a guy, call him. Don't be rude, return his calls...you don't have to do it right away, but return his call! No one likes to be played. I think games are just a waste of time, and they never work for me.

Rule # 15 Don't rush into sex...

Yeah, like I'd follow this rule. I want to know what I'm getting into before I'm stuck with it forever, especially after the feelings get in the way and cloud your/my judgment. They actually want you to wait, wait for a commitment of some sort, or wait for blue-balls or something fun like that. They believe in the philosophy of "Why buy the cow when the milk's for free?" But I can't imagine dating without sex...where's the fun in that?

And my favorite:

Rule #31 Don't discuss the Rules with your therapist...

Their reasoning is your therapist might tell you *The Rules* are manipulative and dishonest...well, maybe that's because THEY ARE!

Those are just a few that bother me, but they also go into what you should wear, how you should have your hair, etc. How can they not know that everything they're advising is all about tricking and trapping a man into a relationship? I've got to hand it to the authors though, they've sold a lot of books and made a huge amount of money. Clearly they have touched a nerve with tons of single girls headed down, not the marital aisle but the spinster canal.

As a single girl in her late twenties with no prospects of a relationship in sight, I am always on the receiving end of either really bad and/or totally odd advice. Cheryl, an older Beverly Hills divorcee, told me to go to the airport and pretend I'm taking a flight, that way I can meet rich business-men flying in. It might be a little harder now that airport security is the way it is, you might just have to hang out in baggage claim, not as elegant of a setting but might work all the same. I should mention that this par-ticular divorcee is engaged to a very cute man half her age, so something worked for her; however, she did *not* meet him at the airport.

After 30 years of living in the United States, my mother's attitude toward men is still FOB (Fresh Off the Boat). And she is full of very bad advice too. She is always worried that I'll scare a man away by, well, by being myself. Like that's such a bad thing. I don't think she realizes how many men I turn down (or don't turn down) and I am always "myself." I can't imagine what my numbers would be if I pretended to be a totally sweet and innocent pushover.

Mom also is always telling me, "Don't show them you're smarter than them." Or, "better than them at anything." Basically, she thinks that I should be, I mean act like, a helpless, overly-dependent, dumb girl who waits on her man hand and foot…yeah like that's going to happen…except for my moments of unintentional domesticated acts. Give me a break. If a guy can't handle me being smarter, or stronger, or all around better than him, then I wouldn't want to be with him anyway. Luckily I'm attracted to very intelligent men who are smarter than or equal to me. Or very stupid men that don't notice I'm smarter than them, so generally it's not too much of a problem.

In general I'm thinking I should stay away from advice from "old" chicks. One old lady, and I mean old, told me I should lie about my age, especially since I am now 29 and almost over the reproduction hill. She thinks men would think my biological clock is ticking. If they think that, they also probably would think all I want to do is settle down, get married and start shooting out kids. Anyone who gets to know me would know *that* is the farthest thing from my mind. I'm 29 years old and getting older every day, and I'm proud of it, damn it, with no desire for kids anytime soon…if ever.

I say always be yourself. I figure if a man doesn't like me for who I really am, I wouldn't really want to be with him to begin with, right? Why fake it? Eventually the real you is going to come out, and if he doesn't like what he sees, I don't think a ring is going to keep you happy, unless your plan is to get married and then get 50%. Otherwise, if you're looking long term, truth is always the best method in my book.

10

THE ONLY RULES, MINE!

I have my own set of rules. I have not religiously practiced or preached these rules, but I think I'm going to start following them very soon; maybe you should too. If you do decide to make these rules your own they might actually keep you out of trouble—or at least out of heartbreak which is much more valuable.

RULE #1 Don't date sleepwalkers.

Being the cool chick that I am, and having the endless nightlife that all hot single girls in LA have (again, with the sarcasm), I watch a lot of *Court TV*, *Discovery Channel*, *A & E*, *The Learning Channel* and my new favorite, *BBC America*. My favorite shows are *Forensic Files, The System, Forensic Detectives, FBI Files, City Confidential*, etc. You get the picture. If a guy really wants to have sex with me, he needs to set me up with TiVo and DirecTV.

It doesn't get me any dates, but I sure am learning a lot about how to NOT commit a heinous crime. But I've also learned that if you date a sleep-walker, they're more likely to kill you in your sleep and get away with it.

More than one man has killed his wife and claimed it was a sleepwalking incidence and left the courtroom a free man. I'm narrowing my chances of being murdered by my loved one if he doesn't already have a plausible defense.

Crazy I know, but I never claimed to be sane. Then again, I have to have some standards, no matter how weird.

Also included in this rule are men who talk in their sleep and those who act out their dreams. Even though it can be funny and interesting, it's just too dangerous. I dated a guy who would talk throughout the night AND he acted out his dreams. So, if Robbie was having a fight in his dreams, which was often, he would basically be having a fight with me. Luckily, Robbie wasn't always that strong when he was asleep, but he did spit at me once. I tried waking him up once. He grabbed me, tried choking me and then put me in a headlock and threatened to kill me. When Robbie woke up he claimed he didn't remember a thing, even after I showed him the bruises. It wasn't fun for me, plus he never said anything good or juicy during nightly conversations...nothing that was a turn-on either.

RULE #2 *Don't date drug users.*

In reality, I probably should say, "don't date drug addicts;" you can't throw a stick in this town without hitting someone who does drugs. I used to be very strict on this, but it seems 9 out of 10 people at least smoke pot. I mean even old people do it...a lot. I've hung out with 40- and 50-year-old potheads...a very scary thing for sure. Old people getting stoned and getting the munchies. I've always thought of it as an adolescent drug, but I was so WRONG.

If you're like me, never done drugs or really been around them, if you meet a guy when he's high and every time you see him he's high, then you think it's his normal everyday personality. Like an idiot, I never quite connect the dots...to me they're just hyper and poor. I've tried to educate myself on what drug induced behavior looks like. I am sure that in my stupidity I will date more addicts in the future, but I will try very hard to avoid this FOREVER.

RULE #3 *Don't date men with children.*

I don't want to be the step-monster of any bratty kids. They'd hate me anyway. My parents divorced when I was in high school, and I'm sure if my father had remarried when I was young, I would have been the biggest bitch on the planet to my stepmother. Lucky for her, they didn't marry until I was in college. I was, however, a complete pain-in-the-ass to my stepfather, but he was a bigger pain in mine.

Then again, dating a man with children may be the perfect solution for me, if he already has a couple of rug rats in the mother's custody he may not try and force me to have any more with him. Then again, knowing me, about that time I would change my mind and want a couple of my own. Just my luck, he doesn't want any more and I'm desperate to have babies.

I, shockingly, did break this rule for a man with three children, from two ex-wives. But, his kids were across the country in New York, so I was pretty much in the clear. I told David that if the kids lived in California it would probably be another story. I don't think he liked that very much, but I couldn't lie. I think David wanted someone who was a little more enthusiastic about his offspring. So, as usual, my honesty was my downfall

RULE #4 *Don't date anyone mentally insane.*

There can only be one crazy person in a relationship at a time, and that is generally me. Two insane people in a relationship make an asylum—not a happy couple.

I know I'm kind of mentally unstable, so if I date a guy with a split personality or some other mental condition, then it would just be a train wreck waiting to happen. I know I need someone who is stable and strong who can keep me in balance and as sane as I can possibly be. Misery loves company, and so does insanity.

RULE #5 *Don't get involved with cops.*

Cops are nuts, power hungry, gun toting meatheads, and they think they're invincible…and I have found that three of my ex's from high school and college are now cops. Guess I'm attracted to power hungry nuts. Surprise, surprise.

When I first moved to Los Angeles, I was on the freeway and a cute cop pulled up next to me. He smiled. I smiled back. And then, to my surprise, he pulled me over. I initially thought it was flattering, but I was so naïve. I should have been scared of him using his power for his own benefit. We talked for a minute then he asked for my number. I still hadn't found an apartment yet, thank God, so I gave him my pager number.

We spoke once before I left town for a quick vacation, Rick gave me his office, cell and pager...but not his home number. I told him I would be out of town for about a month and to call me when I returned. While I was gone, I received numerous messages and pages from him—sometimes up to five or six a day. Most of the messages scared me, Rick would talk about how I was dressed the day he met me, and would insinuate a future physical encounter. I never returned any of his calls. I figured he was psycho, not to mention married since he never game me his home phone. If he was this aggressive pre-sex, I couldn't imagine what would have happened if I'd slept with him.

RULE #6 *Don't date actors.*

In any other city that might be an easy rule to follow, but in Los Angeles you can't cross the street without meeting an actor. And sometimes they're just too cute to turn down. Besides, I love a good tortured soul with an impossible dream that I can try "saving."

There is certainly a personality type for actors...it's what I call the "Me! Me! Me! The-world-revolves-around-me" personality. Beyond narcissistic. The instability. The vanity. Don't get me wrong, some of my best friends are actors. I love all of them. But come on, I can't date someone who spends more time in front of the mirror than I do. Anyway, there can be only one narcissist in my relationship and that's ME!

I did date an actor once, for a few months. Todd told me that he would never come out and tell *anyone* he had a girlfriend, especially directors, agents, managers and casting directors...especially female or gay casting directors. Lucky for me, he also said if they came out and asked, he would admit his relationship status. Todd said if they knew he wasn't available it would hurt his career, so he'd go on "dates" with chicks, gays, or anyone in the business that could help his career. After working on a set, Todd mentioned that the female director LOVED him and that he would be going to coffee with her if she called.

A few weeks later the director called and Todd went to coffee with her. I was okay with the "date," until after when Todd said, "She asked me if I had a girlfriend, and I said no." I was shocked, not only had he lied to her, he'd lied to me! Then Todd swore he would never sleep with any of them…like I'd believe that. I got the idea Todd would do about anything or *anyone* if it meant a part in a movie or TV show.

RULE #7 Don't date smokers, especially chain smokers. YUCK!

They spend more money on cigarettes than anything else, they smoke at all times, including in the middle of the night out in the rain, and not to mention, I don't like making out with an ashtray and having sex with a man that wears Marlboro Light cologne.

My ex-boyfriend, Kyle, would wake up in the morning and light a cigarette—first thing, smoke it, then light another before he even got out of bed. It got really annoying; I think that his true love was a carton of cigarettes. How can a girl compete with that?

RULE #8 Don't date criminals.

Convicts. Ex-convicts. Criminals. Juvenile delinquents. I have enough trouble dating men who don't break the law for a living. I can't imagine what that relationship would be like.

Me: "Honey, what are you doing today?"

Him: "Oh, not much, heist a truck or two, embezzle some money, nothing new."

Me: "Oh that's nice dear, call me when you get home so I don't worry."

I did date a man who wasn't a hard-core criminal, but whenever he went MIA there was always something seedy going on. More than once Joe disappeared for longer than expected and when he resurfaced it was because he had been arrested. On one of those occasions I got a phone call from him at four in the morning needing to be picked up from the local jail. He would have called sooner, but he didn't know my phone number and it took him a while to figure out which was me in the white pages. Lucky for him no bail was needed; otherwise Joe would have sat in that cell for more than just a few hours.

RULE #9 *Don't have sex with your neighbor.*

Never ever do this. The last thing you want to do is run into somebody you've had sex for the rest of your lease. The awkwardness. The weirdness. This is the one rule, I would *never* break. Yeah, right.

I've lived in the same building for more than six years. After a couple years, a cute actor moved in next door. At the time I lived with my boyfriend, so the neighbor and I became friends, but when I became single, the flicker of sex was in the air. It didn't take long to cross this line and break two rules at the same time.

After one uneventful evening out on the town I came home to a party at the neighbor's. Peter was entertaining and wanted me to come over; one of his friends was cute so I agreed to hang out. By the end of the night Peter and I were dancing in his living room and making out. Around 4:00 a.m. the party was winding down, Peter asked me to leave my door unlocked so he could come over later, I agreed. We had mediocre sex and then Peter went back to his apartment across the hall.

It wasn't fun running into Peter in the hallways for a while. Not to mention that I ruined my chances with any of his cute friends.

RULE #10 Don't break the rules.

Rules are kind of stupid and I need to stop making them until I can learn how to not break them. Unfortunately, if I don't at least have some sort of guideline to follow I'd probably sleep with just about anybody. There's got to be a reason why I'm still single, besides my being a completely insecure nut-job, right? I now assume it's because I continually break my own rules.

So that's it, my 10 rules. It's not like they've been carved in stone and carried down the mountain or anything. But they are good to keep in the back of my mind when I meet the *man of my dreams* who happens to be a retired cop turned actor, with three kids, who chain-smokes, lives next door and is so insane that he takes anti-psychotic medication.

11

IMPOSSIBLE FRIENDS

I absolutely love men. That's probably why I'm so easy. Of course, I have had moments of hating them with a passion, but I can't help it, I generally love them.

I love that they aren't catty like women, and in general they're just a lot of fun. I love the way men smell. I love the way they feel. I love how they always want to fix things…you, your car, your problems, everything. I love how they like to feel like they can take care of a woman—friend or wife. I love the way they think. And everything I do is about making myself a better catch, or lay, for the right guy.

I think I've loved men from the minute I was born. I've always been a daddy's girl and a tomboy. I didn't play with dolls, and I loved hanging out with my two older brothers and their friends. It didn't help that I grew up in a town of about 300 people until I was ten. I was the only girl in my class until sixth grade when my family moved to a metropolitan city of 1000 people. I was much more comfortable with the boys than most of the girls I went to school with. It was just a natural fit: men and me.

That ease with men quickly became a hindrance. When I attempted to be friends with the girls in my classes, I realized that I didn't fit in. Backstabbing freaks! It's only been in the last few years that I have created friendships with women that are very meaningful and irreplaceable. It's not been out of a want, necessarily, but more a need. I need to have more than just men friends. It's a need because many of my male friends (excluding my gay friends) were becoming attracted to me or vise versa. There always seems to be an imbalance in a male/female friendship.

My male "friends" are always telling me that I am naïve when it comes to men, especially when it comes to hanging out with male friends. I have always believed, or at least hoped, that there is no hidden agenda; that men and women are perfectly capable to go out and have a good time without any "weirdness," without any sexual tension.

But it has finally sunk in. As I have gotten older I have realized that it may not be possible to truly be friends with a man unless there is no attraction whatsoever for either party involved. That's probably why I have so many gay guy friends. Most gay guys love hanging out with women. Plus, you can flirt with them with no commitment and they'll flirt right back; getting that male love that you can't ever get from some guy you're sleeping with. Best of all, when you're out with them, they'll tell you when you're being checked out by the hot single guys…with absolutely no jealousy. You can't get that in just any friend. And most of my gay guy friends have better taste than I do, so that helps, <u>a lot</u>.

I recently counted how many guy friends I have that I haven't slept with, not including the gay or married ones. That grand total is a whopping two (we're talking friends, not acquaintances). I'm sure at the rate I'm going, I'll soon have no men in my vicinity that I haven't had sex with. I should just ask prospective male friends to have sex with me when I meet them; get it out of the way so we can get on to being real friends. I think the average guy would be open to that, especially since men generally can compartmentalize sex vs. love better than women, or at least better than me. And, if I were to initiate sex knowing it would be just a one-time thing it might be different. I would be narrowing the odds of getting hurt or screwing up a friendship down the road.

I guess there is one problem with that approach, what if you like having sex with that person? Can you truly be friends if you continue having sex with that person and just be friends, no strings, just benefits? I did that once, and it didn't work out very well. I acted like a chick. Got emotional. Got attached. Got demanding. Got bitchy! After 11 months of sleeping with him, hanging out with him and his friends, and talking to him daily I got a little attached, I couldn't help it. I ended the so-called friendship and the sex, before it was too late for me to get out. The only thing I walked away with was that I know I'm one of the <u>best</u> he's ever had. He may not think I'm old enough or stable enough in my career, but I know that I blew his mind…literally.

Someday, I hope that being a very sexual being and having male friends won't conflict. Maybe when I'm 80, wearing Depends, drinking my meals through a straw, and washing my dentures in a cup, I'll be able to have a normal friendship with a man. Knowing my luck I'd end up with a guy obsessed with getting a blowjob by someone who didn't have any teeth…wait, isn't that a common fantasy for men? Then I'd dump him for a hot male nurse who sponge bathes me on Fridays. Until then I'll have to settle for women and gay guys to gossip with and share my tragic love stories…not such a bad fate.

12

MEN ARE PIGS, BUT I LOVE SAUSAGE

*M*en are pigs, but I love them anyway, I really do. I don't think that I could live without them, sexually or otherwise. Men suck pretty much for all sorts of reasons but they're the best alternative out there to being celibate and single <u>and</u> horny. I guess I will have to put up with them forever.

Sometimes my problem is that I sleep with a man that I don't want to get involved with. We hang out, have sex, get closer, but the "relationship" is doomed from the beginning because he was never right for me AND never wanted anything from me except sex.

The problem is I can't resist a man with a cute smile and a cute ass to boot. Men are my kryptonite, my weakness, and my downfall. They're manly. They're hairy. They're strong. And I love them all…figuratively of course. I should be able to blame this all on my father…I'm a daddy's girl through and through. I just like being around men…I can hang with the guys drinking beer or watching sports or talking about cars or whatever. Yet the bigger the jerk, the more I'm "in love." The harder to get, the more I want him.

I mean come on, the other day a guy asked me out to dinner and then the next time I see him, just hours later, I meet his girlfriend. Then, the next thing I know when she's in the other room he asks me out again. If you're going to cheat on your girlfriend don't make a move when she's around, especially after I've gotten to know her well enough not to hook up with her boyfriend.

I guess it's really not their fault; it's in their genetic make up to want to sow their wild oats with as many women as possible. Monogamy is hard for anyone, but if your dick is doing all the thinking, then I can't even imagine what having the same vagina over and over again does.

I can't tell you how many married men have hit on me…probably more than single available guys. Married guys think they have nothing to lose ego wise since they know they have their wife to go home to. If they strike out with me it doesn't really matter. The weird thing is that I always look at a man's hand to see if there's any ring in sight…I really do try to avoid the taken man like the plague, but I seem to attract that type a lot.

As the saying goes, "You can't live with them, and you can't kill them!" What's a horny girl to do?

Part III

13

THE LIST

I keep a running tab of the men I sleep with, a lot of women do. It's kind of childish, but it's fun too. The first time I did 'The List' in college I thought I remembered all of my encounters, but for the next six months I kept remembering the less memorable and "the long ago." I don't know if it was purposeful denial, but eventually I remembered them all…I think. I hope. I lost that list a long time ago and had to reinvent it just a few years ago. It was much harder the second time. That is why, generally, I add them to The List immediately. Currently The List is separated into three categories: pre-college, college, post college. It's long and just getting longer. Yippeee!

To make it onto my infamous List there must be full-fledged intercourse. The Bill Clinton version of sex, of course. Touching, petting, and masturbation do not make it; nor does nudity or oral sex alone. Although, my List wouldn't be much longer if it included such things because I figure if you're going to fool around, have a full night of foreplay, and do everything under the sun except intercourse, you might as well just do it! Go on, add them to The List.

In my mind, oral sex and other non-intercourse activities are just as personal, just as intimate, as intercourse, maybe even more so…to have someone's face in your crotch is a pretty personal, yes? I know that some women can sleep better at night knowing they didn't fuck a guy they just met, but it's certainly okay to put a his dick in their mouth.

I used to work with a girl who was a "virgin" until she got married. Never mind that she was a total blowjob queen, dick tease up until that point. I can almost guarantee that those types have probably given more blowjobs to random guys than I've slept with. I have more respect for women who have safe responsible sex…than for those who are a big old tease.

I told one of my best friends that if anything ever happens to me (death or dismemberment) she *has* to break into my house before my family gets there for three very important reasons: to take anything she wants; to get any "toys" I might have lying around; and, most importantly, to get The List. Her first response was asking me if I wanted her to destroy it. I told her of course not, I wanted her to frame it. At the rate I'm going it will probably be my biggest and only accomplishment. And, it might shed some light on my life for some of my family and friends who really don't know me that well.

Thank God for repeats and regulars, otherwise, I'd be more than just easy. Case in point, I used to date a Frenchman, Pierre. We had an amazing sex life, and that's all we really had, but we had it often.

I ran into Pierre about a year after we broke up, I knew he still had a thing for me so I tried staying away from him. I ran into him at a bar one night when I was out with my girlfriends. He was all over me from the minute he saw me. He told me he loved me. I told him, I wouldn't go home with him because I didn't want to hurt him and that if I did go home with him it wouldn't mean anything, just sex. That, and I drove that night, so I had to take my friends home. I couldn't just leave them stranded for a booty-call.

Pierre was very persistent, and I was very weak. He was so good in bed that I was having a hard time saying no to great sex AND to the convenience of not adding to the List. He offered to pay for my friends' taxi home if I would just sleep with him. So after leaving my friends with enough money for another round of drinks and a ride home, we drove back to his place. They were happy, and so was I. Except that I learned my total value (in Pierre's mind) is only $50. That was the last time I saw Pierre, I don't think he really could handle it just being sex; either that or he just couldn't afford me.

When I think about The List I think I might actually be a slut since I can't remember the names of all the men I've slept with. Some are simply denoted with their occupation or their most defining feature. There's "Freshman dorm guy," "Mexico vacation guy," "the stalker," "Mike, the nurse guy," etc. Someday I'll make a plaque to commemorate all of the men I've remembered and forgotten, kind of like the Vietnam memorial, but until then, I'll just have a note card or two.

Through my influence, more and more of my friends are creating their own Lists. Talking about mine definitely gets them wondering how long their Lists are too, and if they can remember all of the people they've slept with. It's a great girls' night of drinking wine and trying to formulate the Lists. It's a challenge I always put to my friends, especially those claiming their lists are longer than mine or drastically shorter. Most of them don't remember all of their partners either. But, so far in my circle of close friends, no one has surpassed my list...but one is closing quick. I better get to fucking *more*, fast.

14

ONE NIGHT STAND

I sometimes wish I were the type of girl to pick up a complete stranger in a bar, take him home, fuck his brains out, and then send him packing. That is my definition of what makes a one night stand. Unfortunately, I am not that type. I like to get to know a guy for a little while before I sleep with him, unless I'm drunk of course, then it doesn't really matter; but since college, that doesn't happen too often.

My lack of one-night stands only means I'm very selective and picky in very weird ways. I typically pick the biggest loser or jerk in the place, and then I have sex with them before I consciously realize he is a loser or a jerk. Of course on some level I always know what I'm getting into when I sleep with a guy, because if he were nice I wouldn't want to sleep with him anyway. Simple, isn't it?

I have had very few one-night stands, but that's mostly because I believe what's the point of doing it once when you can do it twice? That's why I have so many repeats and regulars, that and I have a very specific definition of what does and does not qualify as a one-night stand. I have these very specific parameters mostly because it allows me to have a guilt-free conscious…and it works pretty well. My definition of what a one-night stand is NOT is as follows:

1. If I know him prior to sleeping with him it is NOT a one-night stand…even if we never have sex again.

2. If you exchange phone numbers and actually speak to each other after the fact it is NOT a one-night stand.

3. If there is an attempt at a second round, even if it doesn't come to fruition, it is NOT a one-night stand.

That's it, pretty basic really. And if I go by it *exactly,* I haven't had any. I've definitely had a few that come close…but it's a little fuzzy. Two happened fairly recently; one with a man that I would never want to have sex with again, and the other with someone who attempted to see me again but the effort wasn't really worth it. I met both of them through friends and hooked up the night we met…which happens sometimes. It's easier to trust a guy won't be a complete freak when you meet him through friends, but it seems that lately they're even freakier.

The unfortunate thing about not being a one-night-stand-kind-of-girl is that I don't know what to do when I'm in what I call "dry docks." Thankfully it doesn't happen very often, so when it does, I just keep my eyes open for a good opportunity for a sex buddy or at least someone I can have a repeat performance with. Everywhere I go I'm looking for my next conquest or fling. I have nothing against people who are able to have TRUE one night stands, I'm actually a little jealous of girls who can fuck a guy who they know they will never see again. They're probably having even more fun than me…and that says a lot.

Again, that's why I keep repeats around for so long. I just rotate new ones in and old ones out. It keeps it fresh and prevents a lot of attachment, especially when you're sleeping with more than one person at a time. However, I may, for research purposes *only,* really work on experiencing a 'real' one-night stand. Next time I'm out I'll have to check out the hottest guy in the place and see if he's game. I'll let you know how it goes. What I won't do for the sake of literature—and education.

15

CYNICAL JADED HOPELESS ROMANTIC

*C*ynical jaded hopeless romantic. Oxymoron? Yes. True? Yes. I am all of the above. I'm not really that much of a cynic, more of a realist I think when it comes to relationships and men. I believe in divorce. I believe that nothing lasts forever. I believe that you can get bored with the one you're with, and that it's okay to want to move on. The hopeless romantic in me believes that if and when I do finally fall "in love" it will be an amazing and wonderful thing and when it happens, I'll know in the deepest part of me.

Most men stay in relationships for fear of hurting someone, or fear of losing their kids, or, more than likely fear of losing HALF. Why not walk into it knowing you've got a seven to 10 year life expectancy on your marriage? Get a prenup. Be prepared. Plan on being back in the dating scene eventually. Stay in shape so when you do land in the singles scene you don't look twice your age and act like a big old geek.

By nature we are not monogamous, right? How can I expect a man to be faithful when I doubt my own ability and desire for just one man? Emotionally I only want one, but physically I have never really been able to be completely satisfied with just one.

The hopeless romantic in me believes that deep down I really do want a modern day romance with the man loving me dearly and sweeping me off my feet forever more. But my conscious is always bitter and skeptical and my subconscious hopes that I am wrong. Completely and absolutely wrong.

These traits are inherent…my brother and I are a product of our upbringing and a little genetics. It really isn't our fault we think the way we do; we watched our parents be a couple. Actually, we watched our parents be miserable. My brother never wants to get married, nor does he want kids, sounds familiar, huh. But, we really can't help it. I'm trying to work through it, and I guess, in his own way, he is too…all the while torturing his girlfriend with hope, no hope, hope, no hope because I think deep down he would like it to work out. He just doesn't think so. Hey, he might just be a hopeless romantic too; he just isn't willing to admit it.

I hope for fate. I kind of believe that everything happens for a reason, and I hope it works for me, really I do. I hope that there is someone out there made for me, like a missing piece, and when we find each other we'll just fit perfectly. Two broken pieces working together. God, I can't believe I just wrote that mush. That's pathetic, but I have to finish the thought. It won't make sense at first, but it'll feel perfect. I hope there's a man out there who is worthwhile and trustworthy that I could actually love, and not just want to be friends with.

I want to be swept off my feet, courted, wooed, loved, pampered, and forced into a happy relationship. I figure if and when love hits me, it won't be my choice. I'll have absolutely no say in the matter, which is a good thing because I'd just find some stupid reason to ruin all hopes of it working out. I'm sure any prospective Mr. Right is running for the fucking hills by now and if he's not yet I'm sure he will be by the end of this. But I can't help being who I am and feeling the way I do. Relationships suck, but I hope they really don't.

16

WANNABE DATING

*I*s there a Prince Charming? If there is, I don't think he lives in Los Angeles. Maybe Prince Charming's manservant, but definitely not the Prince himself. Los Angeles, California, is the land of the wannabes: actors, writers, directors, producers and even wannabe sugar daddies. It makes dating a lot different here than say Walla Walla, Washington, or Poughkeepsie, New York, and a little different than say Seattle or Chicago or Boston. However, every town or city may have one common element, everyone who isn't in a relationship wants to be dating…that is if dating didn't suck and wasn't so hard.

I truly believe that there is nothing wrong with being single. It's actually a lot of fun at times. The freedom. The sex. The variety. But I'm just not good at the whole dating thing. The thing is, I really do want to be dating, and single would be much more fun if I could date well. It's tough being 29 and single in LA…its probably tough being single everywhere I suppose. I'm always in search of friends who might have an eligible hottie for me to be wined and dined, and hopefully sixty-nine'd, by. Unfortunately, that's not usually the case…it's more likely they have a friend that I'll end up just fucking and not get so much as a Big Mac out of the deal. At least I'm getting a moment of pleasure, rather than being bored out of my mind, sitting across from some guy talking about himself all night long AND not being the slightest bit attracted to him; wondering how I'm going to get out of kissing, or fucking him, good night.

I've had more than one friend move from Los Angeles to the East Coast, stating that one of the reasons for the move was that she didn't think she'd be able to meet a good man here in sunny, Southern California. And after the move, they have found it much easier to meet and actually date men. Some of them go on REAL dates at least once a week...that's unheard of here in the "land of dreams." No matter how beautiful or smart or wonderful or whatever a girl is, it's hard to meet a man who's worth giving your attention too.

I've got to give the men in Los Angeles a little credit, if I had to continually approach and get rejected by some of the tactless women out here I don't think I'd ask too many girls out either. I'd settle for the easy girls who just put out without any real investment or commitment. It's much more uncomplicated and not nearly as demanding. Even though I have been known to be demanding on my fuck-buddies, it's never as bad as the nagging girlfriend routine.

The women in LA are tough! But if a guy is genuine, then he won't mind breaking the ice and jumping through a few hoops before we give him a chance, right? He's got to prove he's not lying through his teeth like all those men out there who have taken their dating advice from Lycus 101...not that I object to Tom Lycus, you know, the radio talk host who advises men to do anything and everything to get a woman in bed...and on the top of the "anything" list is LYING.

The thing is, a man doesn't have to lie to get us into bed, at least not lie in the "traditional sense." All a man has to do, if they're not a complete troll or idiot, is be nice. Pretend you're listening. Tell us you like our shoes and that our hair smells good. Tell us you're attracted to us and that we're pretty (caution—be realistic, we know when you're full of shit and only complimenting us to try and get in our pants). Be as genuine as possible. That generally works for me, and if there is any spark of attraction then you'll be in. Unless your mark for the night is a cobweb whoring prude, then nothing you say or do will get them in the sack.

But, the loser-dating environment may partially be our own fault, ladies. Our toughness or bitchiness or skeptical nature could have created the atmosphere; the atmosphere where only idiots would be dumb enough to hit on a beautiful Hollywood Hipster or aspiring starlet or temperamental talent. So the egomaniacs and Napoleon complex freaks are the only ones willing to brave the bitchy storm in hopes of a few phone numbers or better yet, a roll in the hay. And since they are the only ones making any effort at all, 9 out of 10 times they will succeed, sending their egos into an even higher stratosphere.

Los Angeles has what I call the "Kamikaze Dater." These men (or boys) go out to clubs knowing they are going to either crash and burn, which is normal, or claim a rare victory by getting some chick into bed. These kamikaze guys generally go for the best looking, most out of reach chick in the joint...and those hot chicks out there know it's coming. They may not know what or who, but deep down they know they'll have to repel some creep who thinks he's God's gift to women. The kamikaze generally targets a girl in a group, that way he can make an even bigger ass of himself. She, the target, is initially polite, but must resort to bitchy behavior to keep the man at bay. She is usually successful at destroying the kamikaze in a blaze of fire, leaving no dignity...thus becoming the Bitch of the Bar.

It doesn't help that some of the women in this city choose their dates by picking the bigger paycheck or bigger screen credit or better car, instead of dating the man who earns the paycheck, deserves the credit, or earned the better car. Or it could just be that we're a bunch of bitches, drawn to the city of dreams in search of ourselves and men who can handle us...never quite finding anyone good enough.

It's a vicious cycle...if we're too nice, men can and will take advantage, and if we're too mean men get afraid or timid. The men who actually take a risk generally only ask for you to meet them for drinks, or sex as the case may be. Rarely does a man actually ask you out on a "proper date." He's got to test you out first on drinks to see if you're date deserving and worth it enough for dinner...that is if he can actually afford to take you to dinner.

Everyone I've ever met in Los Angeles lives for their work. Work is their life; it's all anyone really has. Most of my jobs are 12 hour a day jobs, and that's nothing compared to the people who work on television and movie sets, 16 hour days are the average for them. I guess that's one reason why so many singles date people they work with or meet on the job...or in my case, sleep with people I work with.

When we're not at work, the odds are we're at an event networking, socializing, schmoozing...I really hate that. Talking to people you wouldn't normally be talking to, except for the fact that they might be able to help your career. It's something you have to endure, because when you're somebody, people will be talking to you because they think you can help their career. It's not really conducive to the whole dating scene but sometimes you find someone worthy to shag.

My lack of dating isn't helped by the fact that I'm an extroverted hermit (I know, it's an oxymoron) and would prefer to be by myself, or just with friends, than going to bars hoping to get picked up by guys. I do get out a lot actually, but I sometimes despise the entire process. I haven't been to too many bars or restaurants that are conducive to meeting a man who's not just interested in sex. What's a girl to do when she doesn't know how to meet a decent guy? Do what I do: go out, meet complete losers, hope to turn it into something or at least get a regular sex partner out of it, wait until you're sick of each other, then wash and repeat.

Proof of the screwed up LA dating scene is the fact that I can go about 100 miles out of town and I get men following me around stores, buying me drinks, approaching me, talking to me, etc. The men outside of Los Angeles are either braver, or just plain old stupid. Either way, it's great, except that fact I don't do long distance.

I do have another theory on why it is so hard for the two sexes to find successful long-term relationships. We all have unattainable expectations. We want super hot, intelligent, funny, rich, successful AND loyal; and that just doesn't exist in men or women. We set our sights too high and from there we can only be let down. Maybe we should look for cute, dumb, not too hairy and fairly faithful and work up from there.

It's bad here but I haven't given up hope on L.A. Even though it's a narcissistic community, at least I'm attempting to date within my "species." I think I'd have the same dating problems anywhere. I've got bad taste and that quality will follow me where ever I go. I'll stop whining about my lack of dating, at least I'm getting laid, that's more than most, so I really shouldn't complain should I?

17

A
DYSFUNCTIONAL
DATER

I am a dysfunctional dater. I just do not know how to date properly, and in the rare instance I do finally get asked out, I just screw it up by either getting bored too quickly or by getting overly enthusiastic, smothering him and losing myself in the process.

I blame my mother. The minute my mother became single after her divorce from my father of over 20 years, she started dating like mad. I couldn't keep track of all the guys she was dating…really, everyday there was a new name added to the phone list. But I don't think she slept with any of them until she narrowed it down to one or two, she just let them wine and dine her until she made a decision. That's probably the key, don't sleep with them while dating them…leave them hanging. Get to know them first, then reduce it down to one, and then fuck them. Nah, I don't think that would work for me…I'm just screwed.

Some of my girlfriends will go out with a guy just because it's a "free dinner." This enables them to date more than one guy at a time and get a free meal. I just don't understand that, I can buy myself dinner. Don't get me wrong; I enjoy the company of a man. When I'm on a date, I prefer to have him pay for dinner, but it doesn't always have to be the case. I will not waste my time or his if I am not at least a little interested in him romantically…free lobster or not. I can always take my ass to Red Lobster for surf & turf.

I think one of the reasons that I have bad taste and bad judgment is that I didn't have much practice when I was a kid. I had a lot of practice in sex, but not dating. I grew up in a very small town in Washington State, with a population of about 1,000 people. It's located near Walla Walla, Washington, famous for its onions, its prison and, my favorite, the fictitious "Walla Walla Acme Company" from all of the Road Runner and Wile E. Coyote cartoons. It's where Wile E. always purchased his weird contraptions. It's surrounded by farm towns including my little town and filled pretty much with rednecks and hicks.

I never fit in, I was always a big city girl trapped in a small town. Not only that, my family was virtually the only minority family…lucky for us we were cute, athletic and smart for the most part. Those attributes worked in my brothers' favor, but pretty much against me. Small towns SUCK. The small town gossip mill is a big part of why I don't know how to date. If you went to the movies with one guy, it practically meant you were boyfriend and girlfriend. But if the following week you hung out with another guy, by Monday you'd be a slut…whether it was true or not. Since I already had a reputation, it wasn't hard for people to believe the worst about me. Unfortunately that kept me from learning the dating basics, which wasn't fair.

When you go to a high school of less than 80 people your dating options are very restricted. Luckily, at times, the surrounding small towns intermixed, but when there is virtually no public transportation system between towns, the only way it works is if you date someone old enough to drive and who has a clean car. That's a desired quality everywhere I think, but in my town you kind of had to worry whether or not their vehicle would smell of farm animals.

Not to mention that I had two older brothers, both of whom slept with more than half of my friends and, worse yet, both of whom kept their friends from dating me. Not from trying to successfully sleep with me mind you, just from respectably dating and courting me. That's probably why I slept with a lot of them, to get back at my brothers, to prove to them, and myself, that I could do whatever I wanted, when I wanted.

The dating pool was significantly narrowed, forcing me to date someone younger than me who was too dumb to be afraid of my brothers. That was until one of my brothers cut his throat a little with a beer can ripped in half after we were caught in bed together at a party. The injury didn't leave any permanent damage—it barely bled, but the rest of the boys in the entire county took that as fair warning to not get caught with me. It also didn't help that my father told my hopeful suitors that if they hurt me he'd kill them with one of the many guns from his collection, which of course he made sure to show every single guy who walked into our house.

Everybody hates dating it seems—unless you're a true player—dating and romancing just to get someone in the sack. I have learned that I am not a player at heart but desperately trying to learn. I think the only reason why people continue to try is that it beats being alone, and it may beat settling for someone you really don't love, or want to have sex with regularly.

Settling is not in my blood, not for jobs and certainly not for men. Observers may think that I settle, but it really isn't settling, it's just my bad taste that makes it look like I'm settling. That's actually an advantage to having bad taste; everyone knows why you end up with losers and freaks. I told one of my freaky boyfriends once that there could only be one commitment phobic person at a time in a relationship, and I was there first. I had dibs. I guess that statement of fact didn't help our relationship, but after he convinced me to date him, which no one could figure out why, he was the one wanting to back out.

And for all of the other dysfunctional daters out there like me, I don't really know what to say, other than, good luck to you…I hope you're able to date loads of eligible men who are willing to buy you dinner before they see you naked, that's the least you deserve…believe me.

18

A PROPER DATE

I must say, I'm a great catch, whether anyone knows it or not. And so are my friends, but we couldn't get a real date to save our lives. I'm not talking about meeting someone for a drink, but a real proper date. Not drinks. Not lunch. A real date, something to look forward to and get real excited about, that's all I want once in awhile…not just twenty minutes of sex, but a whole evening of verbal foreplay.

My ideal date situation would go something like this: I'd meet a guy out on the town or through a friend. There would be a spark or we'd talk. He'd ask for my number, and I'd give it to him, but only after telling him, "I normally don't give out my number, but for you I'll make the exception." He'd call a couple of days later, waiting the proper amount of time, not too short, not too long. He'd ask me if I wanted to go out to dinner Saturday. I'd say yes. I'd start looking forward to it. Ask my friends what I should wear, maybe go shopping for something smokin' hot. Saturday would come, he'd call to confirm. I'd get ready, he'd come pick me up promptly as promised. We'd go to a nice restaurant—his choice, then we'd have a fabulous dinner and some good conversation. Sparks would fly…probably because I'd be tipsy or on my way to drunk.

After dinner, we'd drive back to my place. He'd be a gentleman and walk me to the door. At this point he'd, I hope, give me the kind of a good night kiss that would give me goose bumps. I would, at this point, not be satisfied with just a kiss, invite him in for a drink. I'd throw on some of my get-it-on music from Frank, Louis, Etta or Chet. We'd have another drink, and then we'd make out, a lot. It wouldn't end there...then, we'd have a marathon sex session of course. I know I'm living in fantasy land...I know that the above scenario isn't very likely...well the going out, getting drunk, inviting the guy back to my place then sex is VERY likely, but the rest isn't. But I can dream, can't I?

A while ago I was complaining to Martin, a guy who I thought was interested in me, that it had been forever since I've been on a date, like six or nine months ago or more. Actually Martin would be in the "Nice Guy" category if it weren't for the fact that he's been really inconsiderate. Anyhow, Martin asked me out on a "proper date." He said he'd pick me up. We'd go to dinner. He'd pick the place. Etc. I told him I'd love to go out with him on a proper date...and I waited patiently for the blessed event.

That was almost four months ago and we haven't gone out on our proper date yet. I can't even go on a date with a man who's already asked me AND I've already said yes to. What is that about? I even ran into Martin about a week after he asked, and he looked at me as I was leaving and said, "Proper date?" I nodded positively. Then NOTHING. Not a date. NOTHING. More than three months go by and no mention of it...it's not like I haven't spoken to him or anything. He calls, we talk, but no date.

Martin actually asked me to go out with him again recently, I asked whether it would be drinks or lunch, I didn't want to assume that this was our "proper date." His response, "How about sushi and drinks?" I said OK. It was Friday and we planned to go out the following Thursday. I looked forward to it. I was excited about it. I even planned what I would wear, something I rarely get the chance to do.

The following Thursday came around and I hadn't heard from Martin. No confirmation, no reminder, nothing. I was annoyed. I wasn't going to wait all night so I decided to leave town that evening for a few days. I finally heard from Martin the next evening when I checked my email. He had sent a message claiming he lost my phone numbers...I have to mention he hadn't sent the email until 8:30 P.M. on the night we were supposed to go out, but I still gave him the benefit of the doubt, even though he didn't deserve it...at all.

It was Wednesday of the following week when we spoke again; we made plans for Friday night. I was skeptical. I asked him to call me on Thursday and let me know either way, since I would assume it was tentative until I got confirmation. On Friday, I finally heard from Martin—at 6 p.m.—he left a message saying it wouldn't work out that night either. I'm not quite that dumb.

Too bad Martin didn't take me out on a proper date, it had been so long since I'd had one, that I'm pretty sure I would have put out. His loss. I don't know if Martin is going to be getting another shot or not, however, I do have bad taste and judgment so I'm guessing I'll be seeing him again. If he does get one more shot, I'll have to be tough and make him jump through a lot of hoops. Make him really suffer before I let him take me on a proper date…AND I'll be picking the restaurant, and trust me it will be expensive.

19

MATCH THIS

I know a lot of girls claim they are loser magnets, but I truly am Queen of the losers. I got confirmation of my royal status after trying an online dating service. I'd never tried one before and wasn't sure if I should begin this last desperate route of attempting to meet good men, just so I can reject him or be rejected. It takes so much effort and planning; I didn't know if it would be worth it. You have to put up a picture. Write a profile. Answer a bunch of stupid questions. Going to a bar and getting drunk and letting some guy hit on me is much easier and probably more successful…at least in the immediate gratification department.

It seems like everyone is using this modern day technique, but nobody really wants to admit it. That's because no one I know has actually met anyone worthwhile online and have it last more than an initial date or two. I was sent a free one-week membership around Valentine's Day a few years ago to an online dating service; it was perfect timing, since I was feeling weak and lonely due to the Hallmark holiday. I originally decided to do it as a joke, you know try it out, it would be research and at the very least I could make fun of it a little. Yeah, that's what all the girls say. Deep down we all hope that something like an online dating service will hand us the man of our dreams or at least someone decent enough to have sex with.

I posted my profile with a couple of pictures for seven days. I browsed the profiles of the men in my area, but I didn't contact any of them. I rarely ask guys out because I like being approached; I have an insane fear of rejection. I am relieved that I am a girl and don't have to make the first move too often. That's why I generally give a guy who makes a little effort a chance. It doesn't mean I'll sleep with him, but I'll definitely talk to him to see if he's interesting enough. He's got to get past the initial pity conversation on his own merits.

Not making the first move also includes not initiating online contact. I don't even want to put myself out there for someone I'd never have to speak to. It's probably one of my last old-fashioned ideas about dating, not such a modern girl after all, huh? I mean, who wants to put herself out there for public humiliation, even if the only public is me and the guy on the other end of the Internet?

After my profile was up for a few days, I was flooded with responses. I eagerly opened each email, looking forward to the pictures and profiles of my potential future mating partners. I couldn't have been more disappointed, mortified or shocked. I thought I'd at least get responses from men who walked upright and didn't live with their parents. I was so wrong. For a minute I thought I might have logged onto the wrong dating service, In-mates R' Us, or something of that nature.

I realize there are a lot of people out there looking for love, and I think it's great that they're trying, but for the love of God, try reaching out to someone in your own hemisphere before you try outer space. I could not have been more traumatized by the responses my profile and picture received. The few that I decided to at least email back didn't really follow-up. Again, the whole thing was such a waste of energy and time. I was definitely looking for Mr. Good Enough in a pool of crap.

The one 'date'—and I use that term loosely—was when I met one of my matches out for coffee one evening. I got dressed for the occasion. I looked great, if I do say so. Skirt. Cute sweater. Make-up. Etc. Jerry however showed up in jeans, sweatshirt, and white sneakers. Not to mention that in my profile I said I wasn't interested in anyone over 40. He was 43 and I was making the exception, but come on, first impressions make all the difference. I never saw him again. A little phone tag but that was it. I took my profile down before the week was up…I'd had enough with my online experiment.

I'd rather be celibate than try that again. The only other dating service I would even consider is the Millionaire's Club. The membership fee for men is $10,000 to weed out the non-millionaires but for the women it's free. I actually downloaded the rules and forms from their online site to see if it's something I might be interested in. What stopped me was the application form; it advises you that by applying you consent to be used in their advertisements. That scared me, the last thing I would need is be the poster girl for marrying for money through a dating service.

Unless I try another online or dating service I will have to resort to the traditional method of dating and getting laid. Make myself as available as possible to the existing men in my life, and wait around for someone to introduce me to the man of my dreams. If that doesn't work, drink myself silly until the ugly troll starts to look like a Prince Charming, then take him home and have a nice little romp, until I wake up the next morning with a headache and a hairy guy named Chet laying next to me.

20

GULLIBLE TRAVELS

I am so fucking gullible, way too gullible for a girl who's pushing thirty. It makes me sick, it really does. Sell me a bridge, or tell me you like me and don't want to JUST have sex. Unfortunately, I put trust in people who are undeserving and tend to be skeptical of anyone really sincere.

I broke *the* cardinal rule, the rule that's so unbreakable it should just be called a "given" rather than a rule: never, ever sleep with a man that you're friends with first…if you actually like him *and* are attracted to him. It will always end in disaster, no matter how good he is.

My feelings got in the way from the get-go, influencing every move, every thought. I warned myself off of him for months. Eddie wanted to date me; I told him I didn't want to date him. I told him I'd destroy him, that I'd just use him for sex. Of course, I was more afraid he'd destroy me, and that I would *really* fall for him; which I did.

Eddie told me he would fall in love with me if I let him. I believed him. Eddie told me he loved me. Ask me if I believed him. Go ahead, ask! "Did you believe him when he told you he loved you?" Of course I did. We started spending all of our time together.

He asked to borrow some money for his cell phone bill. I loaned it to him. He told me he'd pay me back when his check cleared. I believed him. I later found out he was borrowing money from me to buy drugs. But here's the stupid thing (since it's all been so normal so far): it wasn't the last time I loaned him money. I'm an idiot, I know. Even more ridiculous, this wasn't the last time I loaned a guy money. I'll never learn. Maybe I'm not gullible—just stupid.

I can't help believing in the so-called "good" in people…I think it's the small town girl in me just trying to get out some way some how. I don't think I'm alone. I think many of us want them (men) to be honest and tell us the truth, the whole truth, nothing but the truth. We don't want to believe that they are lying. We don't want to believe we are being used for sex. We don't want to believe that we aren't interesting. Because if we think they're lying then it means that we are being used, that we aren't sexy and irresistible, that we aren't interesting, that they will pay us back.

For my 30th birthday, I would like someone to give me a little skepticism and a little doubt. You'd think my jaded cynical views would translate into this area of my life. Apparently my habitual bad habits are not lessons for improving that part of my life, only ruining it. If only I were as trusting in great guys as I am in morons.

21

WHAT'S YOUR SIGN?

T he best pick up line is no line at all. But if you must, PLEASE be original. Seriously! I'm not sure why men use lines. If you need some sort of line to start the conversation just make sure it's not completely idiotic. Why would someone want to talk with—let alone have sex with—someone who is completely unoriginal?

I slept with a man once because of my girlfriend Frankie, well, probably more because of a line. I have a set of Frankie's keys and she had a friend who needed to stay at her place while she was out of town. She called to tell me to meet this friend at a neighborhood bar to give him the keys. I agreed to meet up with him, mostly because for years she had talked about him, how cute he was and all, but I never met him because he lived out of town. Shortly after meeting him and a few drinks and a little flirting, the dialogue went something like this:

> Freddy: Frankie's bed is really comfortable.
>
> Me: I've never slept on her bed.
>
> Freddy: You haven't? Maybe you will tonight!
>
> Me: No, thanks.

Guys who assume I'll sleep with them are a big turn-off; nevertheless, I slept with him that night. I'm terrible at saying, "No." Freddy was a bad addition to my List because it wasn't that good. He wasn't a great kisser and he had a big penis that he didn't know how to use. It was such a complete waste of time.

I guess the line worked, even though it's not the only reason I slept with him (remember, it's really Frankie's fault). But his line let me know that he wanted me. If there was any doubt, he made sure there wasn't any. That and he kept buying me drinks, which always help.

While I was in college, one of the best lines ever used on me, or at least the one that I'm most fond of, was while I was at a phone booth (obviously this was prior to the rampant use of cell phones). A man in a Jeep Cherokee pulled up, oddly close to the phone booth, practically on the sidewalk. I thought he was lost and needed directions. I stepped out of the booth and moved a little closer, not close enough for him to kidnap me or anything, I'm not that dumb, but close enough to help him if he needed it. He leaned out his window and said very nicely:

"If I give you a quarter will you call me?"

I started laughing. I thought it was a really bad line, but for me, and most women for that matter, if you make us laugh you've won half the battle. I ended up going to lunch with Sam that day. I never did sleep with him, even though I saw him a few more times after that. We became friends, which I'm *sure* was why he pulled onto the sidewalk in the first place (note the sarcasm). Men don't generally use their best lines to score another friend, right?

Guys need to understand, if they are hot or I am desperate, then they can say just about anything and I will sleep with them. Actually if a man is hot, he doesn't have to say a word to me. Just a cute little smile and a come-hither look will do just fine.

I haven't had a lot of experience really hearing pick-up lines. But some of my friends use them, and unfortunately many receive them. My friend Lawrence humiliated himself with this one, here's the set up:

A good-looking girl is in the frozen food section, and Lawrence pulls out:

> "Excuse me Miss, you're going to have to leave this aisle because you're so hot you're going to melt everything."

Very funny, but I think it was stolen. It also was in the movie *My Blue Heaven* with STEVE MARTIN who gives it with perfect delivery. If you're not Steve Martin, I don't suggest using it.

Here's another that was actually used on one of my girlfriends:

> "Didn't the doctor prescribe you only one cute pill a day…what are you up to four or five?"

Cheesy, I know, but there is definitely a sweet quality to it.

My friend Allen only likes to date "little girls." Therefore, he generally tries to make sure they are legal first. One day he walked up to a young looking girl…and the following occurred:

> Allen: How old are you?
>
> Young girl: Why?
>
> Allen: Because I'm going to hit on you and I want to make sure it's not a federal offense.

Funny, yes, but I think that would have even scared me. Apparently she thought it was funny too and he got her number!

A horror story from this guy I know, Steve:

> Steve: Hey, do you work out?
>
> Girl: Not really, why?
>
> Steve: Because you look really strong.

She just kind of stared at him for a second. He felt so stupid that he left her standing there without saying a word. He would have been better off not saying anything or just "hi." At least he would have been able to leave the bar with his dignity.

My most recent favorite was from a man I met in Atlanta's airport. He was being made fun of by ALL the other men in the bar for a line he had just used on another bar patron:

Man: (walking up to woman) Has anyone ever told you that you have the most beautiful eyebrows?

Woman: (uninterested) Yes, they have.

She then walked off and left him standing there to be made fun of by the bystanders.

In general, you don't have to do much to get an easy girl to sleep with you. Just be nice and try to be honest (well, that works for me anyway). But you do have to sound genuine.

When I was 18, I quit college within the first 5 days...I panicked. My mother wasn't too happy with that decision so I had to go live with a relative and her new husband Jared (who I'd known since the eighth grade). It was an ideal situation. Until one day I was downstairs watching TV when he called down to me from the shower, I went up so I could hear him better. This is how it went:

Jared: (Peaking head out of shower) You wanna get in the shower with me?

Me: (freaking out inside) Um no!

Jared: Why not?

Me: (freaking out even more) Because you're married to Sherri!

Jared: She doesn't have to know.

I told Jared I would forget about what he'd just asked if he would too...Give me a break! Gross. I'm not going to sleep with a blood relative's husband.

My advice to the men out there, know when to give up…if it's a lost cause try to salvage your dignity and what little self respect you have left. AND don't hit on anyone in your wife's family! If we think you're hot, or cool, or whatever, all you have to do is say "Hello." Nothing else needs to be done to break the ice. We really have heard it all before. However, if you still feel the need, please try to be original and/or exceptional. If you use a line, use it with confidence, use it with style.

Part IV

22

TWO FOR THE ROAD

*T*here's nothing worse than a happy couple when you're single, horny and lonely. They just rub it in your face. The kissing. The handholding. The cuddling. The secret language. The happiness. Yuck. Just kill me before I hit on your boyfriend or throw-up on your shoes. Couples just plain SUCK. You know you think the same thing too…just admit it, you'll feel better.

And don't even get me started on being half of a miserable couple…ick. They're weird. They're boring. They dress alike. It's just awful seeing two grown adults dressed like a western blanket, wearing matching bolo ties and doing the electric slide. Shouldn't there be some sort of intervention or something when couples do that? Start dressing alike, looking alike, talking alike, acting alike…keep a little of your own identity please! If I ever wear a matching outfit with my significant other, unless it's for Halloween or some other valid function, you can kick me in the ass AND tell me how stupid I look. Please!

Another part of the nightmare is the endless dinner parties with the same people week after week. The same couples week after week. Couples named "Todd and Keri" or "Jennifer and Steve." All of them driving mini-vans or station wagons and clipping coupons and having "game night" just trying to relive the fun of being single but not even coming close. Zombies, going through the motions…shoot me before I start playing Yahtzee or charades on a Friday night!

Then again, if you're not part of a couple, then you're probably forced to participate in couple's events. It's just the same boring couples having the same boring conversations about their kids or their dogs. And the singles are forced to pretend you care about whatever the boring topic of the night may be…car insurance, topsoil, car pools. To make the evening worse, they either have invited, in their minds, another lonely person they feel would be happier if they found someone just like you. Or, worse, they continuously hound you about your single status, making stupid statements like, "A girl like you shouldn't have any problem getting a date." Which I like to follow up with, "I don't have a problem getting a date, I just have a problem keeping them around after the sex." Do I need to spell it out? I L-I-K-E B-E-I-N-G S-I-N-G-L-E! That should eliminate any confusion don't you think?

I'm forming a group called SAAC, Singles Against Annoying Couples; we'll meet on Saturday nights…it'll be like a date, but more fun. Either no sex or a lot of group sex…maybe we'll turn it into a sex club and kill two birds with one stone.

My ex-boyfriend Hugh is always *trying* to set me up, but never actually succeeding. Nevertheless whenever the occasion arises, he tells me about a guy he knows, or someone his girlfriend knows. Why do they insist on forcing their lifestyles on so many of us? Is it the misery loves company philosophy? The more couples there are the more, the more they feel like no one should be single. The more people that are doing the same boring things that they do, the better they feel about their own pathetic lives.

I know I'm kind of a hypocrite in this regard because whenever I find myself as part of a "happy" couple, I find myself in conversations like:

Me: "Honey bunny, can you get me a glass of water?"

Honey of the moment: "Of course sweetie puss."

(Kisses)

Me: "Thank you punkin'…you're the best."

Honey: "Not a problem lover bear."

(Kisses and maybe a wink)

Me: "I love you snook-ums'"

Honey: "I love you more!"

Me: "No, I LOVE you more!"

Honey: "No, I LOVE YOU MORE!"

(MORE SICKENING WET KISSES)

My vocabulary begins to consist of things like "Okay Honey bunny sweetie pie punkin' bear." Or when I'm on the receiving end of, "You're the bestest my love angel," "You're my pumkin' patches," "My princess," or "Thank you honey bunches," I become what is the most annoying of all. I become that most hated thing to unhappy singles everywhere…the giver and receiver of much PDA (Public Displays of Affection to those not in the dorky know…but I actually think it's so lame to refer to it as PDA.). You can officially kick me for even knowing such a term.

When in a couple, I participate in Public Displays of Affection everywhere. It makes me sick to my stomach sometimes at the thought of how "cute"…and I mean that in a bad way…at how cute of a couple I've been a part of so often. Maybe it's because I, at times, enjoy being a part of couple, being in a relationship…I know, I know, I'm a hypocrite. But since I'm generally only part of a couple for about three months, max, I try to annoy as many bitter singles like me as I can.

It happens to me all the time, forced to witness the annoying behavior of happy-touchy-feely couples everywhere. And, I can't forego this irritating opportunity because I never know when I'll be a part of a couple again. It could be years before I'll have the opportunity to rub it in the faces of singles and unhappy couples everywhere…I've got to make the best of it while I can. What's even more fun is rubbing in the I'm-getting-even-more-frequent-sex to the sexless singles and abstinent prudes.

Luckily I don't have any close friends who are married and only a few who are even part of a couple, so I'm rarely forced to do the awkward couple thing. Being alone is very underrated, damn it. But as long as I'm not part of an unhappy couple, or a settling couple, I don't care. I'd rather be alone than settle for a relationship, settling on a man who isn't right for me. I'm bitter, I know it. I admit it. But that's OK...I've come to terms with my bitterness and when it's your turn to be single, you should too.

Being single means that I can wear what I want whenever I want. I can be selfish. I can be self-involved. I only have to worry about me. I never have to worry about making someone quit smoking or making them pick up their dirty underwear or whatever annoys me about them. On that note, I do have to say that you shouldn't get involved with someone knowing you want to change him (or her) or expecting him to change something you don't like. People don't change, especially if they don't want to...and most of the time people DON'T WANT to change. So, all of you who are a part of a "happy" couple, if you met the person and they smoke, don't try to make him/her quit. If they bite their nails, don't expect them to stop. If you want to control someone or be their boss, start a business or have a kid, spare your prospective mate and us single folks from dealing with the misery of you.

23

HELL HAS A WHITE PICKET FENCE

*T*o love, honor and cherish…in sickness and in health…'til death do us part. Yuck, right? I know there are others who feel the same way. I'm in total fear of commitment and of letting someone in who might possibly hurt me. But most of all, I'm in total fear of being bored to death in my 'normal' life and waking up to someone who annoys me more than anyone else in the entire world.

My commitment-phobic brothers and sisters know what it's like to be judged for their lack of nuptials, their lack of desire for the old ball and chain, the car pools, the commitment. We're ostracized from our community, our family and our committed friends. We are faced with the looks of, "Why haven't you settled down yet?" "What's wrong with you?" We are many! We are strong! We are tired of being judged. And we are probably all a little bit jaded, but we want to come out of the commitment-phobic closet with our heads held high and say together, "I don't want to get married! And that's OK." Deal with it.

I do…actually I don't. Weddings suck! There's no way I'd ever get to the picket fence because I could never get through the I do's. And I have some experience there having had the misfortune of being a part of more than my fair share of wedding parties. Torture! The ugly dresses. The waste of money. The relentless planning. The over-priced dress! I could buy a kick-ass wardrobe for the price of a wedding dress. I'd rather elope to Vegas or have a small beach wedding, and then rent out a bar on another night and have a raging party/reception with all of our friends…bringing presents of course (not that I've thought about it mind you). I've witnessed too many women stress over the planning and seating arrangements and flower girls and the appropriate hairdo's…so much that they don't even enjoy what's supposed to be "their" night. Give me a break…I had a girlfriend who was given the choice by her father of a big wedding or he'd buy her a house. She chose the wedding. Ten bridesmaids. TEN. I would have been house hunting instead of dress shopping immediately.

My sister (who is happily working on her second marriage, has a two-year-old and is working on a second rug-rat) mentioned recently that I am single with no prospects of a real relationship. One word came into mind, "duh!" but I don't care, marriage is the last thing on my mind. Sure, once in awhile, when I date a halfway decent guy, or even not so decent, it crosses my mind, but there's no picket fence or mini-van in sight for me.

I dated a guy who said he wanted to marry me. I believed Aaron meant it, I just didn't believe it would actually happen, and I was right. Especially when he said he'd have to date me for 10 years before we'd ever get married. My response to that was what's the point if you wait that long? Just for that little piece of paper? For the legal record? It's not like I'm going to be changing my name, so that's not a good reason either. I have no interest in being referred to as Mrs. Dumbass or whatever my Mr. Wonderful will be named. When a man takes a woman's name without any regard to the name she's had all her life, then I'll consider changing mine. Until then, I have and always will be Angel Adams, thank you very much.

My fear of commitment and marriage is partially because I don't want to wake up in a suburban nightmare…house, picket fence, two kids, a dog and a husband who, if he isn't cheating, is probably thinking about it…a lot. Now that's what I call hell. I know parts of that is some girl's dream situation, minus the philandering husband, but that is far, far from my dream. I think my dream situation would be to meet a guy who respects me, cares for me, believes in me, trusts me, and loves me as much as I do him…and on top of this mutual satisfaction, we'd have a great sex life of course. Perhaps being able to live together without wanting to kill and torture each other everyday. That's all I want, if and when I do meet a guy who's worth hanging out with for more than six months.

I'm lucky one of the many loser guys I've totally fallen for over the years hasn't actually wanted me back. I'd probably be strapped down with a ring from Sears, a whining brat kid and a double wide trailer…cookin' my dirty ungrateful man dinner and running around in lingerie from K-Mart trying to get him to notice me and not the television…that is if I even still wanted to have sex with my bum of a husband. By then I'll probably have abandoned all hope and relied on a couple of rechargeable C-size batteries as my life mate…thanks Duracell.

It really doesn't help that I think every relationship will eventually turn to crap—marriages included. I know that's no way to go through life, but I can't help the way I feel. Almost every relationship that I thought was going well has turned to crap. Not to mention that so many married and/or committed men have hit on me. Men who've just met me and have been married for 30 years coming on to me in a hotel hot tub. A relative's husband telling me he'd leave his wife for me if I'd have him. A stranger in the car next to me looking for a hook up on a Saturday afternoon. A college friend on a business trip. A married boss wanting a blowjob…you get the idea.

It also doesn't help that I grew up in a house where at 12 years old I heard my parents say they'd just stay together until I graduated from high school. At that point I wished daily that they'd get a divorce and stop the fighting…I mean come on, why torture yourself and your kids by staying together for all of the wrong reasons? My advice, don't get married and avoid the whole messy affair. Either that, or believe in divorce, plan for it. Because unfortunately the odds are it will happen. But don't jump ship at the first sign of trouble. Jump only after you realize you hate the person you're waking up to everyday—then you must leave.

Carson, a guy I was sleeping with, who had a girlfriend I might add, once told me that I had a "flashing green light on my forehead" and that's why he made a move on me. Well, as for the flashing green light, I guess I am always open to adventure, but just because it's there doesn't mean you should make an inappropriate move. Carson was making moves. I mean, we were sleeping together for almost six months before he and his girlfriend broke up. Even though I wanted him, lucky for me, Carson didn't want a real relationship with me when he broke up with her, he just wanted to continue fucking me…oh and be my *friend*. Yippee! That's all I need in my life, another guy I've slept with to be my friend.

For every married couple out there, I hope that it works out for you, I really do. I hope to be proved wrong someday. Not just by the couple who stays together and doesn't cheat, but by a HAPPY couple. And when I say happy I'm not talking about content or staying-together-for-the-kids kind of happy. I'm talking about in love and happy and having fun and still wanting to have sex with each other and not completely despising each other every day; still kissing, making out, and really loving each other. If you're out there and have been married for more than ten years please call me and let me know…I want to study you, figure out what makes it work. Not as a science project but because I've never seen it, and I want to.

24

GENETIC CODE

*T*he pitter-patter of little feet. Babies. Kid-litts. Munchkins. Aahhh they're so cute, they're so adorable, oh give me a break, really they're just little adults. Little helpless needy adults, with no money. Rug rats. Blah. Children. Ick. Babies. Yuck. Dirty Diapers. Yuckier. The crying. The endless crying. The expense. The pain. Not to mention the weight gain. Stretch marks. Saggy boobs. Loose vagina. Mommy body. Are they really worth it?

Oh c'mon…I'm kidding…a little. I'm not really that vain but I would like to stop MY genetic code now! Stop the madness. My sister and brother are already contaminating the world's gene pool as it is, I don't need to be passing on my own psychosis to an innocent, unsuspecting child. I wouldn't mind passing on my great personality and sense of humor of course but that's ALL I want to pass on. I have control of stopping my genes from going any further, and that's what I'm planning on doing. One less messed up kid in the world the better, and I can almost guarantee that my child would end up messed up, the next OJ Simpson, the next Heidi Fleiss, or the next wart on society.

Don't get me wrong, I love kids…as long as I can give them back at the end of the day. I was the youngest of four growing up and never had to take care of any babies. I never baby-sat kids as a teenager. I worked on a farm; I drove a truck and drank beer with the boys. No babies. No kids. No diapers. I never had to deal with that sort of thing. I've probably changed three or four diapers in my lifetime, and I wasn't too happy about any of those times either...hopefully, I can go another 30 years without changing any more. If they're not yours you can hype them up on candy, spoil them rotten, and then send them packing back to their parents to deal with the bouncing off the walls and the temper tantrums.

Anyhow, if I have a kid, I'd probably have to get married and live that suburban nightmare life I dread so much, since I think one of the main reasons people get married is to have a family. Then again, it's probably a moot point anyway, I don't think any guy would really want a kid with me...he'd be crazy or a saint? And if me being nuts doesn't scare him off, the negotiations before any unprotected sex would surely send him packing. Adoption, caesarian, nanny, housekeeper, personal trainer, big house, no breast feeding, boarding school optional, etc...all part of the unbreakable contract...no loopholes just pure, undeniable demands. Oh, and most important, the 100% guarantee that he'd never ever cheat, and will still find me very attractive and sexy even after I get my mommy body with the ever-special and attractive stretch marks. Even if I lose my sex drive, he'll still have to adore me, otherwise he'll have to suffer, in a way no other man has had to suffer before, for the rest of his life. Too bad there's no legal way to take a man's soul...that would be the best contract of them all...have a kid, sign over your soul. Simple enough!

I think all women should have such demands, call it a 'preconception agreement' to go with the prenuptial agreement. I'm sure the lawyers will be all over this concept, another way to make their $500 an hour. Just imagine the ambulance chasers and the power attorneys fighting for this unlimited source of business working to create an ironclad contract binding the father to be the best there ever was. Don't get me wrong, I would never want to stay in a relationship because of children. Nor would I ever decide to be with someone for a child.

I guess that's another reason why I don't want children at this point in my life, mainly for the fear of how it would change me. I'd become all mommy-like. Of course, I'd be a MILF (Mom I'd Like to Fuck), but I'd still be a mommy. And it would change my relationship, that is if the father sticks around, the child would become the focal point of every moment...and you have to remember it's all about ME, not some kid.

Rug rats! Who needs them? If I need to hear the pitter-patter of little feet, I'll get a kitty-cat to keep me company…and I'm allergic to cats. What does that say about my desire for children? Pets are much easier to get rid of than children…you can return a dog to the pound. But what are you supposed to do with a kid? Are they worth the 18 or more years of responsibility? Eighteen years of emotional torture and torment…I think I could die happy without all that. I'm almost thirty and still a huge pain in my parents' ass…I can't imagine what my kid would be like. How can I commit to a lifetime of being a parent when I can't commit to a yearlong magazine subscription?

Payton, one of my boyfriends, said if we ever got married he wouldn't make me have two kids, but he'd have to insist on at least one. I asked him if he thought he was dating someone else because obviously he didn't know me very well. Payton said, what I've heard a million times from people who discover I don't want children, that I'd "make a good mother." What I want to know is how do they know? What makes them think that I would be good at anything? They don't know that I can barely keep my plants alive, let alone something that lives and breathes and needs attention, affection and FOOD. And so what if I'd make a good mom! What difference does that make in choosing to have a child or not? I'm good at a lot of things I choose not to do. I'll bet I'm a great thief, but I don't do that. I'm a great liar, but try my hardest not to be. What difference does being good at something make? Most people who say this don't know me well enough to make this determination even if it did matter…and it doesn't.

I don't want to be responsible for adding another asshole to the world population. And if I ever change my mind, I would adopt. I don't need anyone to have my eyes or hair or smile or whatever people want to pass on. I think it's selfish…it may be self-preserving, but I think it's selfish nonetheless. You can adopt and be a parent if it's that important to you; there are enough children out there who need parents that are giving, loving and needy.

Maybe I have these opinions because I haven't met a man who makes me want to create something that's part of me and him yet…maybe it's because I'm not old enough…maybe it's really because I'm actually the one who is selfish and cannot give up my own freedom to have a child. Only time will tell…but I can tell you that if I do finally meet someone who changes my mind or I get old enough to hear my clock ticking I will have a boy. Only a boy! I would have to demand to have my man's sperm spun to almost guarantee no females, only males.

Boys seem much easier…the hardest thing to teach them is to pee standing without making a mess and, of course, putting the seat down. I'm sure I'm over simplifying but you get the picture. I was a huge pain in the ass. Girls pretty much suck. And they're so high maintenance…the dresses, the dolls, the prissiness. I was a tomboy, and I wouldn't know where to begin with a 'real' girl. I cut the hair off my sister's dolls when I was a kid. I liked to play in the mud. What would I do with a girl except fuck her up? Not to mention that if I ever had a daughter like me, I'd have to kill myself. There's nothing worse than a strong-willed, bratty ass girl, and that's exactly what I was. Girls are scary. I know this for a fact, I would much rather put up with an ornery boy than deal with a girl's puberty, again. Plus, keeping all those horny guys away from her until she's ready is a task I'm not up too.

Then again, I'm guessing my hypocrisy, or baby clock, will get the better of me, and some day soon I'll realize I can't live without a child and start pumping out kids like a Peez dispenser. I'll be a protective, overbearing, overly affectionate, annoying, PTA leading MOM!

The bottom line is that I will not have a kid for any reason except for my actually wanting a child, knowing I can take care of me and the child, and not being able to live without one, otherwise what's the point?

25

SABOTAGE

sab·o·tage

Treacherous action to defeat or hinder a cause or an endeavor;
deliberate subversion.

I have recently learned from www.dictionary.com that I have mastered the ability to sabotage. Better said, I can successfully ruin a relationship without even consciously trying. I haven't had a boyfriend who has lasted more than three months in the last four years. I've had sex buddy relationships last longer than that, but there's no commitment and no expectations, so it's safe. There's no real need to sabotage a safe relationship.

When I do get in a relationship that seems to be "good," I am always waiting for the bottom to drop out. He'll get bored of me. I'll get bored of him. He'll change his mind. I'll change my mind. He'll wake up one day, generally within the three-month time frame and realize I'm not what he actually wants. Or I'll realize that I was blind or hallucinating when I decided to date him. How can I commit when I expect it to end? I tell myself I'd be stupid if I actually believe the relationship will work out.

My most commonly used sabotage technique is the "smother and run" method. I meet a guy, have sex with him within the first couple dates, that is if there is any actual dates other than getting drunk, making out and having sex. Then we base our relationship on sex, never really getting to know each other, and having the time of our life for, well, about three months. We spend every day and night together, then I wake up one day and realize my needs aren't being met, sexually or otherwise. Let's be serious, the older you get the less men put out, and I decide that they don't even know me, nor do I want to get to know them. So I run, if he hasn't already run for the hills. It's pretty simple really...a guilt free, no effort break up.

I know I'm not the only one who does this, but I think I've perfected it. If only I could bottle the Three Months of Heaven Relationship without any side effects and sell it on the open market to those who aren't too commitment phobic to try but commitment phobic enough to not want an actual relationship...I'd be rich.

Another sabotage method is "the suspicious cheater," this isn't used as much because the relationship doesn't last long enough and I'm normally not too jealous of a person. But I do fully expect the man I'm with to cheat or wish to cheat, so sometimes I become the psycho, jealous, suspicious chick who thinks the relationship is perfect except for the fact that at every moment my abnormal unrealistic insecurities flood the scene. This, at times, causes me, the girl, to act proactively. If I can't catch him in the act, then I'll just go ahead and do it too. I generally never tell the man, but I feel good and bad that I may have the upper hand having done such an immature thing first. The guilt normally gets the best of me and, instead of confessing, I either make up a stupid reason to not see him anymore, or (my favorite method) I'll be distant and act like a jerk picking fights so he'll break up with me...just like a guy. Somehow it elevates the guilt of cheating if you're not guilty of breaking up with the poor guy. He keeps his dignity by saying he dumped you, and you really know why it didn't work out. Everybody wins, right?

The fear is still the motivation. At times, I have a fear of what I am or am not missing out on if I'm in a relationship. I haven't met a man yet who I'm happy enough with that I don't think that. Nicolas, one of my male college friends called recently and we were discussing his recent marriage. I asked him how it was going. His reply: "OK." He's been married for less than six months, and it's "OK." I asked what was up and Nicolas said that he wished he would have gotten married when he was younger so he wouldn't know what he was missing out on. Since most men are getting married later and later in life, I'm pretty sure Nicolas is not the only one who misses his free swinging bachelor life with no one to answer to but himself. I know I would miss mine too if I were all of a sudden married. You can't blame him.

Then Nicolas said that when he goes on business trips now it's even more difficult. There are always all kinds of women around with opportunities to cheat, which of course he thinks about, but right now his morals and commitment are keeping him faithful. Which is a good thing, but how long is that going to last if the temptation is already there after only six months? Within a few years the temptation may be too great, or Nicolas might become that emotionless, zombie husband doing what is right because he HAS TOO! Maybe cheating, maybe not, but certainly not living his life, that's for sure. Always thinking about the happy life that he misses every day of his miserable life. The poor bastard!

I don't want that for my husband or me. It just seems that the amount of time to be happy in a relationship is minimal, so why foolishly think it will be around forever? Why not keep every relationship brief and to the point? Having all the fun you can have, then jumping ship before it sinks. Either that or start drilling a hole in the bottom, like I do, or keep your eyes out for an iceberg and steer straight for it and hope for the sequel to the *Titanic*.

I probably sabotage because I don't know if I've ever been really "In Love." I've said I love you back to a lot of guys who I know for sure I didn't love. I have grown to love some, but I know I wasn't ever IN LOVE with them. I definitely know infatuation, maybe a little too well. It's the best feeling in the world for about three months. Then it disappears about the same time I get dumped or bored

I *am* one step closer to solving my sabotage "problem." I am *aware* of my bad behavior, but, as usual, I am not ready to change. I guess when I do finally get to that desperate point of either dying alone or finding a man to love me and give him a chance, I'll know what to talk to my therapist about. That should be fun:

Therapist: So what's the problem now?

Me: I'm a total commitment phoebe who sabotages any potential relationship before it starts…and now that I'm 50 I've
realized that I want to stop.

Therapist: Then do it, if you want to stop, just stop! Simple.

Me: No, not simple I can't just stop…I don't know how.

Therapist: How does that make you feel?

Me: *(angry, I hate that question)* It makes me feel like crap, I'm
50 years old, too old to attract anyone decent and too neu-
rotic to actually have anyone fall in love with me! I'm
screwed!

Therapist: *(looking at watch for the 100ᵗʰ time)* Well, Angel, that's
all the time for today…next time lets continue on this,
but until then think about how you have sabotaged
your relationships and why.

Me: Yeah, homework…like I haven't already thought about that
before.

I'll make another therapist rich off of my pathetic psychosis and probably
still not be able to commit, but at least I'm trying. I am trying so hard. I'll
never give up, NEVER. Men beware, I'm on the loose and looking for love,
or sex…is there a difference?

26

MARRIED OFF

*I*t's funny in the 21ˢᵗ Century you don't hear about arranged marriages too often, but when society did utilize this method of courting it seemed to work…probably because it had to or the couple had to face their parents' wrath. It's a little better than getting drunk at a bar and looking for some guy to give your number to hoping that six months down the road he'll propose and you'll live happily ever after. I'm sure back in the day my parents would have paid my worth with couple of cows, a pig and a herd of sheep to get me out. I certainly would have been married off to the richest farmer in the village. It's a sad state of affairs that I'm not even worth a slab of beef! When the highest bidder is a guy who doesn't even buy me a drink, I'm in some serious trouble.

Recently I got off the phone with my mother, like that's not trauma enough, but we were discussing the possible marriage of my younger cousin in Vietnam to an American man 30 years her senior. My mom found him in Denver, Colorado, just looking for a young Asian girl to be his house and sex slave. My cousin doesn't even speak English. My mother claims that she knows "Enough!" then revealed that she knows an entire 20 words! 20! My mother thinks that's plenty! It may be the perfect amount for the man, he won't have to talk to her, listen to her or anything…he'll just point at things that need to be cleaned and have sex with her whenever he wants. This wonderful prince charming is going back to Vietnam to get her and bring her here for the wedding. I've never met my cousin, nor her fiancé, but financially this is a good situation for her and she gets to live in the United States like she always wanted. I guess that's why mail order brides are still so popular.

My mother then told me she had an idea. I got worried. Whenever she gets an "idea" it's not good. She said that since I'll probably never get married (WHAT?), especially for love (again, WHAT!), she could have my aunt find me a wealthy Vietnamese man to marry. She even went on to explain that if I *did* get married, I wouldn't have to have sex with him if I didn't want too! Now I know where I get my naiveté from, my delusional mother thinks that if you marry a man for money you don't have to have sex with him. Exactly what world does she live in? A green card marriage maybe, but I don't think that's the kind of marriage he would actually want to buy.

I only live a few blocks from Beverly Hills, so I told her that if I wanted to marry a man for money that I had no problem finding one on my own. That, and I know I could get more than $20,000 for my cock-sucking ass. $20,000 isn't even a down payment…maybe in a few years when I'm a little older and a little more haggard. I mean seriously, if she's willing to sell me off to the lowest bidder then I might as well be hooking my ass on Sunset Boulevard. I'd probably have more fun and get a lot more money for my efforts. Five-dollar blowjobs to celebrities'…mom, if you're going to sell me, SELL ME!

My mother has had some off-the-wall ideas before but that one *really* took the cake. Actually, I'm still in shock. For one, she thinks I'll never get married…I'm not that un-marry-able, right? And secondly, it's not like I'm that old. I still have plenty of time to marry if I want. So what if I can't wear white! So what if I'll need my walker to get down the aisle…I'm OK with that.

Since I have rejected her arranged marriage ideas, I now must convince my mother that I don't need her to think of me every time she meets a single man. I wish she'd stop calling me out of the blue telling me she met three divorced guys that are really nice. Nice? I always ask if they're "hot." This confuses her and she normally responds, "They're nice, I don't know if they're hot." I'm not so hideous that I have to marry for personality…maybe in ten years or so, but even then I will still want smokin' hot with a nice ass as an option. Maybe I should send my mother a "minimum standards" list...she can check things off whenever she meets a "nice" guy at the gas station, grocery store, back alley or wherever she thinks she can find me a quality man.

I really am afraid that the popularity of dating and marriage reality shows will prompt my mother and/or family to enter me as a "contestant" on the "Marry My Spinster Daughter Please" show. Or give me up as the grand prize...or the booby prize as the case may be...in some sort of "Worst Bachelor in America" contest. They'll do anything to get me down the aisle and off the market. They don't care if I skip the dating, courting, get to know you stage, as long as I eventually get the "I do" part over with. They'd probably be happy with "it's nice to meet you...I do!" Luckily, there are already two grandchildren in the family so there's no pressure on me to have children...they know me better than that.

I think what astounds my family most is that I'm not married to a rich guy by now. In reality I think they're not really bothered by my being single...as long as in the end I don't marry someone poor. Of course, I love the tortured soul, poor artist type. They just want a man for me who will take care of me...especially since I can't seem to hold down a job for more than a year. Unfortunately, pretty soon I'll be too old to marry rich. I will no longer be a hot, young, single chick, in just a few years I'll be the aging woman who's never been married and is way desperate to do so.

At this point, I'm almost thirty and haven't been in a relationship forever. My family hasn't even known me to have a boyfriend in almost 4 years. They probably all think that I'm a lesbian or something since I keep turning down all of my mother's long distance match making. I do have to say that if there is anyone actually looking for a matchmaker, I need to hook you up with my mom. She could start her own business (and stay out of mine) and make tons of money. She could support me for the rest of my life and not worry about marrying me off to my own sugar daddy

27

INSTA-BOYFRIEND

*O*ne date does not make a boyfriend. Two dates doesn't either. Why is it that some guys just assume they're your boyfriend just because you sleep with them? I don't assume that some guy I just slept with is my boyfriend; actually I assume the exact opposite—that I'll never hear from him again. Now, maybe if I had a guy take me on a real date, then I might get the wrong idea. But I haven't been on a date in more months than I can count, and I'm way too jaded to assume such a romantic notion might actually happen.

Every "boyfriend" I have ever had has told me he loves me inside six weeks, and I really have never understood why. Is it because they love the sex? Am I attracted to men that love "love?" I've been told I'm a very "loveable" person, but give me a break I know I'm not THAT loveable. It's gotten to the point when a man does say, "I love you!" that I just kind of snicker, and it kind of blows a romantic moment out of the water. Instead of "I love you" back, he gets, "Yeah right!" No wonder they don't stick around for very long, I guess I'm not grateful enough. I know how special it is to have someone fall in love with me, but I just don't believe that they actually love *me*.

Not too long ago this love phenomenon happened again…and I actually hoped it was true, that a nice guy might finish first. Unfortunately, as usual, this is a story of bad judgment. The thing is, I had heard that Harry was a drug dealer long before I ever met him. We ran in the same circles but went years without us ever actually meeting. When I did finally meet him, I asked about the rumors…he said he only sold drugs to his friends. Nice guy, right? How could I not date him? I mean, how could I resist, he's a drug dealer who only poisons his friends…at a profit.

Harry was kind of good-looking, I guess. Somehow he did convince me to get involved with him, even though I protested and said I didn't want a boyfriend, especially one with a very hairy back. I'm not trying to be vain but I don't want to be on vacation and be THAT girl who's got the boyfriend with the fur coat in 95-degree heat. Yuck. And if he wanted it shaved, who do you think would be the one who would have to shave it? Me! I don't think so. I'd rather avoid that situation, but to his credit, he said that once he closed a "big Hollywood deal" he'd get the laser removal. Someday I hope to see him at the beach with a smooth as a baby's butt back, but I have a feeling it was all talk—like everything else about our relationship.

Harry was an "insta-boyfriend." Within two weeks he was telling people I was his girlfriend. I was in shock, but much to my surprise it came off as kind of sweet. I, however, couldn't get the word "boyfriend" out for awhile…he was a guy I was dating but didn't tell my guy friends (meaning my fuck-buddies, for fear of losing them). He made it so much worse when he told me he loved me within three weeks, a record at the time for the fastest anyone had ever said it. Oh, and I almost forgot the most important element of all, Harry gave me oral sex twice, and he didn't do it too well either. The second time around I had to give him some pointers which helped a lot, but I want a guy who really wants to go downtown and once there knows which way the subway goes.

Hairy-back wasn't the only insta-boyfriend. There was the man I call "The Stalker." I met him. I took him home. But, I didn't sleep with him that night. He called me every day until we went on date a few days later. We went back to my place. I told him I wouldn't sleep with him. I only took him back to my place, because, well, I drove; he didn't own a car; and I just didn't feel like driving him back to his place. The next morning I woke up to The Stalker looking for some action. I said no. He persisted. I got bored of saying no and tried to forget the fact I wasn't all that attracted to him, so I gave in, as usual.

It wasn't very memorable sex either, well I remember it was *bad* sex. I finally get him home, but then I started receiving phone calls from him at least once a day, but generally more. Apparently he didn't get much sex, and he assumed it meant we were in a relationship. Well, it didn't! By Friday he became unrelenting and very annoying. He called at 9 A.M., 11 A.M., 2:30 P.M., 4 P.M., 7 P.M., 9 P.M., and 11 P.M., never leaving a message. I don't think he realized I had caller ID, so he didn't know I knew it was him all of those times. It wasn't until 2am that he left a message telling me he was just calling to say, "Hi!" Just a nice little, "Hey how are ya doing?" message—*at two in the morning*. Exactly what I want from a man I just met. I was completely freaked out; he knew where I lived, and I have a very over-active imagination. All I could imagine is The Stalker coming over and killing me in my sleep. Or worse yet proposing to me and professing his psychotic love.

The next day when, of course, he called again I asked him for a favor. I asked him to not call me until I called him because he was FREAKING ME OUT! He politely agreed to my request, and then wanted to know what I was up to and what I was doing later. He had no clue that I didn't want to talk to him anymore. I got off the phone very, very quickly and thankfully never heard from him again…I guess he got the not so subtle hint. Thank God.

It's pretty obvious I'll never be happy, right? When they want me, I don't want them…when they don't want me, I'm all over them. I'm as guilty as all of the guys running around looking for a good challenge. I just need to realize that nothing will ever continue to be a challenge, that's just the way it is. That's life. Most men are a challenge because they don't want me or because they are jerks, and I think I can change them. People never change unless they really want to and from my experience, most people don't want too.

I guess when the insta-boyfriends disappear and I'm left with nothing I will miss them; their eagerness, their annoyance, their unrelenting chase. Maybe the next time an insta-boyfriend lands in my bed I shouldn't be so quick to get him out of my life, he might actually turn out to be the one. If not *the* one, perhaps one who is at least good enough to keep around for a while…you never know where you'll find a diamond in the rough.

Part V

28

BRAGGING RIGHTS

*H*ow many times have you heard a man boast his sexual abilities?

"It'll be the best sex you've ever had! I can guarantee it!"

If you're a man who does this, STOP. We like to be surprised by a man's abilities in bed. Why do you claim this? Is it part of trying to convince us to sleep with you? If I slept with all the men who made that claim I wouldn't be just easy I'd be a complete slut…or whatever it is I'd be.

Every match is different. Chemistry plays a part. Just because some woman told you you're the best *she's* ever had, doesn't mean you are the best for every woman. Last I checked, *People* doesn't give out the "Best in Bed" award. How would the writer make that determination anyhow? Would the journalist sleep with all the men nominated? Would there be an online site so the 40-year-old they de-virginized back in high school could put in her two cents? It could be featured on *Dateline*: "If you've slept with this man, log on to vote if he deserves the Best in Bed award of the year." I could nominate a man or two.

What I want to know is, does the guarantee of "being the best" I've ever had get me the twenty, or five, minutes of my life back if it isn't in fact the best? Or, even better, do I get a certified letter from you saying we never slept together and that you won't have to be added to my List? I mean, what's a guarantee worth if you can't get anything in return if it fails? Maybe the guarantee should be that he, the guarantee-er, must perform sexual favors exactly as commanded until he really is the best I've ever had. And when finally achieving that status, he must continue for at least a month or two…kind of a bonus for enduring through the "not so best sex I've ever had." Sounds fair to me.

I met a male prude once, really, who amazingly made the "best ever" claim, trying to convince me of his manhood and capability. Sean went through his whore stage, claiming he'd slept with more than 200 women. Recently divorced, he only wanted to have "meaningful" sex while in a "significant" relationship. That was a first for me since living in Los Angeles. However, apparently Sean thought I'd be significant enough because he offered it up every chance he got.

He boasted that if I had sex with him it would, again, be "the best I'd ever had." Sean claimed to be able to "cum on demand" too. I really didn't see the extra added value in that but he said he could last for hours until commanded to cum. Sean also bragged of his love for oral sex and how he "never gets tired" of giving it. That was about the only intriguing and desirable quality that drew me to him at first, but when a man says it'll be the best I've ever had, I want not just great *oral* sex but great SEX. I must admit he peaked my interest, but I hear these locker-room claims all the time. It doesn't mean I believe them, and it doesn't mean that I'm going to sleep with them to find out.

Sean, a male prude and not the typical man-whore, did make it a little more interesting than the average guy. It's kind of ironic that he'd become the challenge in a lot of girls' eyes; he was the one girls wanted to use just for sex…mostly because he'd been so adamant about saying NO to women who approached him. Sean believed there was nothing wrong with oral sex, but he drew the line at casual sex, or even a sex buddy kind of relationship, which was the only thing I could offer him the first time he asked me out.

There was a bit of desperation in Sean's search for a meaningful relationship, more than likely he was just horny and the "meaningful relationship" was the only way he had convinced himself he was allowed to have sex. It was, however, kind of nice to see a man with a little bit of self-control and selectiveness. He was not sleeping with just any girl who was willing...not that he didn't go through that stage of no standards and no taste...but he had graduated to a better place. ME!

I did discover that Sean really wasn't much of a challenge at all, nor was he really that much of a prude either. One night he made a move, which wasn't surprising since it happened weekly, and my mind reeled. I wanted to fuck him, I was attracted to him enough and I was horny too, but I knew he'd get hurt in the end. I told him once that I would destroy him if we dated because of my commitment phobia. Sean thought I was scared of him, because he was still claiming it would be the best sex I ever had. Unfortunately, he kept reminding me that he wanted a healthy relationship in the future. As you should know by now, healthy relationships aren't exactly my specialty. So I turned him down, told him that it wouldn't mean anything more than just sex.

A few days later, Sean was a little drunk and while sitting across from me, smoking a cigarette, he said quite matter-of-factly, "I think we should have sex tonight!" I laughed. I was flattered as usual, he thought I was beautiful, but I knew he had a thing for Asians and that always annoys me. Sean persisted saying it was a good idea and that he'd be OK with whatever it did or did not mean. He just wanted to have sex! I didn't want it to ruin a perfectly good friendship, but I figured he was a big boy and could take care of himself. Besides, my conscience was clean...I had given him full warning.

Well, we ended up back at my place and fucked like rabbits—oh, I'm sorry, he made sure I knew that he wasn't fucking me, only having sex. Not making love. Not fucking. Just SEX...apparently there's a difference. I don't know if it was the best I ever had, but it was good enough. Maybe even top 5 for oral, it was fantastic.

He said I was in his top 3, mainly because he claimed he didn't like blowjobs and I gave him an amazing one. I didn't believe it for a minute, but when I asked him why, Sean admitted that only one woman, out of all the women that had tried, was able to give him a good and proper BJ, but even she was unable to give him an ORGASM. He also mentioned that he didn't think most women liked to give oral sex. I had to prove him wrong, of course. I'm proud to say that now Sean likes blowjobs…a lot! And I gave him mind-blowing ORGASMS too. You can never say I am not doing my part in improving mankind. I never boasted once of my ability to give him a blowjob he would enjoy, I let it be a very, very pleasant surprise…as it should be.

29

1-900-SEX-TALK

You ever get so horny that you just have to reach out and touch yourself? Phone sex can be a godsend. What better way to make a solo activity a little better than adding a sexy voice and heavy breathing, a little moaning, some down and dirty sex talk to the equation? Oh, and a phone bill from Ma Bell that could choke a horse? It's fun when you're missing your man or you have nothing better going on, but come on, doing it yourself with only a voice to get you through the night gets old pretty quick.

I had phone sex with Ted, a guy who lived in Hawaii. I was there on vacation, and we went out on a date the last night I was there. We didn't have sex, but we fooled around on the beach. It was pretty awesome, but I wasn't as adventurous back then, and I think I was too paranoid that we were going to get caught since we were right out in front of the restaurant…I'm not much of an exhibitionist. If I could do it over, I would have enjoyed the entire setting and had sex with him.

When I returned to California we began talking on the phone, at first it was "get to know you" type stuff. Boring, but if you ever want to get to the phone sex, you have to get through the dull stuff first. Within a week we knew each other well enough to be much more productive with our long distance dime. Ted had a nice voice, and I hadn't had sex for a little while so it was easy to get me worked up. The great thing about phone sex is you can imagine anything, what he's doing, how he's doing it, etc. And, you've got this great voice on the other end just urging you on. A lot of guys don't talk enough, or at all, during sex. But with phone sex they're forced to, otherwise you'd just hang up. And I LOVE a little filthy talk during sex, more men should do it...if you don't know what to say, just ask!

We had a couple of months of phone sex by the time Ted finally came to Los Angeles to visit; unfortunately, by the time he visited, I was over it and him. I couldn't get him out of town fast enough, it was a complete let down. I didn't even want to have sex with him, but figured I couldn't *not* have sex with him. Especially after he flew all that way to see me, right? After getting him worked up with all the phone sex for two months. We'd already done it in our minds, what's the big deal with our bodies acting it out too? So before he left, and after annoying me for a week, I slept with him. Another notch in the headboard I didn't need.

The sad thing was the phone sex was better than the real sex. When Ted went back to Hawaii, I couldn't have been more relieved. Unfortunately the motivation or inspiration for phone sex was gone. It was ruined...there was no more fantasy, just cold unforgiving reality. It's pretty bad when a man is better over the phone than in person. I was completely disappointed because a good phone sex partner is very hard to find. Plus, I was between live sex partners and that's all I had.

Gwen, one of my girlfriends, found herself in a long distance relationship and had no idea how to begin a long distance sex connection. She was thirty-something and had never had phone sex. She didn't know how to bring it up in conversation, and she wasn't sure if he'd ever reached out and touched himself via a midnight cordless phone chat.

I once had phone sex with a guy right after we had sex. Gabe came over, hung out, had sex, and got his. I didn't get mine. He had to leave right away. I decided to do it myself but was feeling the need for a little help. I just called him up on his way home from my house, not having been satisfied with his visit, and initiated some hot and heavy breathing. It was fantastic and it really helped get me to that massive orgasm I had been craving but was unable to have with him that night. Let me suggest, if your guy doesn't get the job done the first time, try giving him a second chance via the phone. Ah, communication is key.

It's sad really, I can't even remember the last time I had any real good phone sex…I kind of miss it, really. Maybe I should hang out in airports looking for a guy with a nice voice who is leaving town on the next plane. We'd be heavy breathing in no time, maybe I could even get him to call me from the plane. How fun would that be? It's been too long since I've been involved with anyone that's gone out of town, or at least called at the right time.

I don't do long distance well …why reach out and touch someone through the phone when you can reach out and touch someone new and near with your own two hands. It's human nature to look, and if you have someone near and dear to go home to it's easier to look but not touch. I'd be touching all over the place if I was the only one touching me *and* paying seven cents a minute for it too. I'm too needy and too sexual to be satisfied with only phone sex to appease my appetite.

In comparison to other styles of self love, phone sex has to be a thousand times better than cyber sex. I admit it, I haven't really even had cyber sex before. Mostly because it has never appealed to me, and I really don't get it. The first time I was in a chat room and some guy asked me if I wanted to "Cyber," I didn't even know what he meant. I felt so stupid and naïve that I left the chat room never to return again…shamed by my inept abilities, I vowed to return only when I really knew what I was doing.

Besides that, how can you do a really good job pleasing yourself and the person on the other end when you've got one hand down your pants and you're only typing four words a minute, complete with smiley faces and "LOL?" Come on, that can't be that memorable or satisfying. I'd rather be by myself with my toys and some good old-fashioned porn.

Of course, I still choose one-on-one, in person contact over any other. But if there's no other choice, horny, hurtin' for some love, needing a change of pace from the porn and vibrator routine, I'd choose phone sex every time. A sexy voice is always better than interesting fonts. And with speakerphones and headsets, its hands free baby…two hands are always better than one.

30

WET NOODLE

here once was a man from Nantucket, who could not get his penis on up it. I know, it's a very, very bad limerick, but it's fairly fitting for the occasion. I don't know any girl who hasn't experienced the limp-dick, can't-get-it-up, "Whisky Dick" syndrome. It's OK guys, we girls all know it happens…and that it happens to some more than others, unfortunately. It's a sad fact of life when hooking up. But when it happens with a guy you're dating, and it's the only impediment in the way of actually having sex for the first time, it SUCKS. Especially when nothing, not even sucking, can get it up.

It happened to me a few times in high school and college, but luckily only once by each individual guy. Embarrassed and guilt-ridden, they generally prove their worth within 24 hours. Reassuring my feeble ego that it wasn't me, but them. They are generally under some sort of influence, which is completely forgivable…once. It does, however, sometimes hinder the opportunity for a second chance. Girls don't want a limp dick, ever. Not giving a second chance reduces the possibility of it happening again. Ego saved.

Laura, one of my girlfriends, dated a guy who could never get it up. She loved hanging out with Jack, they got along great, but when it came to sex she dreaded it. It was always limp or semi-hard, like soft serve ice cream. Worse yet, Laura would attempt to give Jack a blowjob to help it up…it worked some, but not always. On more than one occasion Laura would be sucking, licking, tugging away and it would just lay there…limp and unmoving. For me, sometimes half the thrill of giving a blowjob is to have it come to full salute while in my mouth…a wet noodle just doesn't do it for most women.

I felt for Laura. And I don't know many who wouldn't. One of my last "boyfriends," Rod, had this problem for almost two weeks. It was so frustrating. The first two times we tried he was drunk…I let it slide. By the third night of limpness, I was ready to just be his friend because it was too aggravating and too much effort. He said it was because he never felt so nervous and excited about anyone the way he felt about me…cute, kind of. I tried everything, and I mean EVERYTHING. Nothing would work for more than a minute, once it was up, it would just go down. It was like a floppy jack in the box, popping up then disappearing from sight…up, down, up, down. I get dizzy just thinking about it.

Like a typical chick, I thought it was my entire fault; Rod wasn't attracted to me, he was gay, or something silly like that. He assured me it had never happened before, excluding the occasional whisky dick. I know at that point it was harder for him because he knew I thought it was my fault. So he tried harder, which didn't produce anything remotely close to hard. It was a vicious cycle. It didn't help that I discovered the first few times we tried he had been on ecstasy and cocaine…I generally try not to knowingly date guys who use drugs, but I really didn't know. That did help explain the first few times, but it didn't explain the days that followed those first two incidences.

What made it worse was that if Rod couldn't get it up, no action could be had for me. He wasn't willing to do anything if it didn't benefit him. It was all or nothing…I'd get all worked up, then nothing. NOTHING! He'd just give up. Wouldn't even try. I sure know how to pick the givers. I should have listened to my instincts because I knew then something was 'off.' Even when his "problem" went away, the foreplay and non-intercourse action was basically non-existent. Being sexual isn't just intercourse; all of it is fun, all of it is enjoyable. If I wanted wham bam, thank you ma'am, I'd just do it myself and save the emotional hassle.

Apparently, Rod was a little concerned about the turn of events too because he had discussed his problem with a friend. He was getting as annoyed as I was. Thankfully, his friend was prepared for this kind of emergency and gave Rod a Viagra. When it finally came down to the wire, he was ready. Lucky for him because I was only giving him one more chance. The pill worked, thank God, and we went all night. It was like unleashing a lion that had been taunted and teased for months. It was a lot fun, and the sex wasn't bad, but I don't think it was worth the wait.

To this day, Rod is annoyed I told my friends about his "little problem." But please, if you can't get it up and you've just started dating a girl, expect her to talk to ALL of her friends. Lucky for Rod, once it was up, it wouldn't go down and I made sure I told my friends that too.

31

GERIATRICS

I love older men. I love men who look like men and not boys. I like older men, not men old enough to be my grandfather mind you, but distinguished men. Unfortunately, older men have the sex drive of a *dead* grandfather. I've never been turned down for sex as often as with older men.

I guess it doesn't help that I have the sex drive of an 18-year-old boy or a 30-year-old woman at her peak. I can't get enough sex. I could do it every day, over and over again. And that scares me. Science tells us that a woman's sex drive only increases. What happens when I hit 35? What then? Hopefully I'll be a 35-year-old hottie who can still attract a hot young legal "adolescent." But what if I'm stuck with a 45-year-old with no apparent sex drive?

I often wonder, "Does my sex drive doom me to have sex with boys who have no body hair and live with their parents?" I'll have to start hanging out on college campuses and under 21 clubs. I'll be that weird old lady dressed funny, trying to be sexy and hip, but not quite achieving it. Or, I start hitting on my friend's kids or nephews. I'll be the "Mrs. Robinson" of the neighborhood. That probably would be better than a future of one-time-a-week, or one-time-a-night sex with men who have little or no endurance, saggy balls, and no sex drive. I'll be the death of older men everywhere. But that's better than having a heart attack while jogging or doing something else not so worthwhile or glamorous. Die while having sex? That's the way I want to go, just not with an old fart. I want to die in the arms of man with a rock hard body and a rock hard cock.

The first time I ever had four orgasms in one night was when I was 27 with a 23-year-old. I'd go back for more in a second, but I don't want to ruin the perfect memory of that night. Tony had endurance. Stamina. Passion. Technique. If only he weren't so immature…something easily ignored for all-night sex and multiple orgasms, just not for a relationship. Not that I would want one. I guess if I want to have great sex with young guys I'll have to get used to the immature thing. Seems I'll have to start playing video games and hanging out in malls so I'm HIP and COOL.

Ah, who am I kidding? I've always been attracted to older men. I'm sure some would say I have a father complex of some kind, but I don't think it's that. Men are men, boys are boys…a lot of men don't grow up, I just happen to like the ones that have, at least a little. I have a lot of girlfriends who think it's gross to date anyone five years older than them…which is just plain weird if you ask me. These girls are the same who think it's gross to date someone five years younger too. Again, totally insane.

I've been sleeping with older men for as long as I can remember. When I was 17, just out of high school, I went to Hawaii with my sister for two weeks. Two days before I came home I met a very nice looking 38-year-old doctor who asked if I wanted to go to the beach and watch him surf. Dr. Parker was cute and older so it was perfect, even though I didn't know exactly how old he was at the time. We spent the day together and ended up back at his house, which was absolutely beautiful and a total "closer." I ended up having sex with him and it was great. I learned then that older men seem to know what they want and how to do it…they just don't like to do it TOO often.

Two weeks later Dr. Parker flew me back to Hawaii to see him. By this time I was the whore of my hometown and everyone was gossiping about my flying off to see some old guy. It didn't matter, I was completely infatuated with my doctor and he was with me. Regrettably, I soon learned that older men really do know what they want, and what they want is to SLEEP. We only fooled around a couple of times during the week I visited him because he was always tired. And when I finally got him to perform, it didn't matter if I got my orgasm or not, he'd be fast a sleep in no time after he got his! Sleep is the older man's priority, first and foremost. With Dr. Parker I think I was tied at third place, with food or work…surfing and sleep came first. How can I compete with such tangible things? I can tell you that every older guy I've dated and/or had sex with has not wanted to have sex even half as often as I do. Everything is a bigger priority than getting it on, and I don't understand that. What's so great about sleep?

I do have to admit, looking back on the "relationship" I think it was kind of sick…I understand lots of men like younger women, whether it's a mid-life crisis or they just want some young meat, but come on, when I was going to recess, he was literally going into retirement, how compatible is that? If a 38-year-old man dated my seventeen-year-old daughter I'd have him shot. I mean I was only seventeen, even if I acted older and looked older than I was, I was still way too young. For some "odd" reason Dr. Parker didn't seem to mind my age…surprise, surprise.

From then on, I learned a valuable lesson, age really doesn't matter but sex drive always does. Men stay child-like all their lives, and it seems that the only real things that change are their income and their sex drive. As their income goes up, their sex drive goes down.

For a while, I was sleeping with Evan, a forty-year-old confirmed bachelor, when we did have sex it was pretty good. It just wasn't nearly as often as I would have liked. One night I told him that I didn't want to be alone: i.e., I'm needy and you'll get sex…any way you want it, and I'll get sex too and therefore be a little less needy and less of a pain in your ass. But Evan turned me down, for Monday Night Football…FOOTBALL. This from a man who claimed I was in his top three in bed, if not number one. I can't say I was surprised, this is the same man who never initiated sex unless high or drunk or both. If I stayed the night with him four nights a week I'd be lucky if I got sex once. That's what I get for sleeping with a forty-year-old guy who smoked pot EVERY day and didn't have a sex drive.

I'm sure my days of fucking old farts aren't over, at times their technique and methods can't be beat, and generally they're great company. Plus, older men generally know how to go to town giving oral sex…some younger men seem to either not like it or have no idea what the hell they are doing. I do seem to be hit on by older men more often; they possess more confidence. I guess the odds of my hooking up with an older guy is greater since young men are just plain chicken.

If I found an older guy, not more than 15 years older than me, who wasn't a commitment phoebe, had an amazing sex drive and/or a prescription for Viagra and wasn't TOO hairy, I'd probably be in heaven. But until I find my mature prince charming I'll just have to keep after some of the young studs out there.

32

THE OLDEST PROFESSION

*C*all me old-fashioned, but I give it away for free. Trust me, I wish I didn't. I'd be rich by now if I charged what I was worth...or at least what I think I'm worth. There's nothing wrong with the women who do it, prostitution or stripping, as long as they're safe about it. I'm actually a little jealous of women who can charge for sex and/or use their sexuality for money...even if it's just having a sugar daddy. Using their body and sexuality for income or power. Bravo!

I had a friend, Rebecca, who had a relationship with a man twice her age. He was unattractive and rich; she was cute with a great personality...you get the picture. She genuinely cared for him, but she wasn't 'in love' with him. He gave her a car, money, and his credit card. Even when the relationship was on the outs he still took care of her. While he stayed in Los Angeles, he sent her to school in New York. He dated other people, so did she. It was the perfect set up, and I was envious. When Rebecca got done with school the relationship was over. No strings. Nothing. How perfect?

When I was 17, I fell 'in love' with a man more than twice my age. All he wanted was to take care of me: move me to Hawaii, pay for my schooling, set me up completely, etc. All I could think was that he wanted to be in control and that, in the process, I would lose control. I was so naïve and such an idiot, I know. If someone who I genuinely cared for offered to take care of me right now I would snap it up in a heartbeat (I hope). So, I'm fielding offers. I've matured, I think, and I believe I could handle a nice rich guy who cared about me and wanted to take care of me at this point in my life...as long as he's cute with a strong sex drive. Or old with no sex drive, and I could try to send him to an early grave...JUST KIDDING. Old guys and saggy balls are not my thing.

If I ever did entertain the notion of becoming a prostitute I would either be a Beverly Hills Four Season's type call girl or a legal prostitute in Nevada where it's regulated. Dennis Hoff, owner of the Moonlight Bunny Ranch outside of Reno, Nevada, once offered me a job to work for him anytime. The girls in Nevada are taken care of and make pretty good money. If you're going to sell your body, do it right and make sure it's worth it. No five dollar blowjobs and no walking the seedy streets of Hollywood at night along side the transvestites and crack-whores.

I have given selling my body for money enough thought that I've figured out that I would have a decidedly different rate sheet than the average prostitute. I would charge a standard high fee for straight sex; additional fees for kinky or anal, a nominal rate for a basic hand job. But, my highest fee would be for blowjobs...which are generally cheaper for most hookers, but for me it's too personal having a penis in my mouth. Your vagina can't taste or smell...having your face in some guy's crotch is another story. I probably wouldn't get much work, but I'll have kept my high standards!

Jon, a male friend of mine who I haven't slept with (yet), is a firm believer in and somewhat of an advocate of making prostitution legal. His argument is that women should be able to do whatever they want with their bodies. If men are allowed to sell their bodies to play on a football field, where they destroy themselves and have a career span of only a few years but make a ton of money, why can't women have the same opportunities? Selling their bodies on the open and legal market for tons of money and probably achieving fame along the way. Just think there could be famous hookers hocking Trojans or lingerie or sex toys on television for millions and millions of dollars. That would be fair. I mean if it was legal then it would be a tax write-off, and I'm guessing some hookers would offer a "buy 10 get 1 free," just like a car wash. Tax write-off and discount sex, what could be better?

I guess for now, I'm going to have to stick to giving it away to all of the unavailable guys I seem to always date. No use changing a system that has worked so well for so long.

33

INCEST ISN'T BEST

My brother's favorite saying while we were growing up, actually he still says it once in a while, is something that has always scared me…and it'll scare you too if you're smart. "Incest is best!" The fact that we are descendants of trailer-trash rednecks makes this an even scarier statement. Doesn't that just chill you to the bone? No? Well it should. It does for me, and I am from the South where this kind of thing is second nature.

I had the unfortunate misfortune of almost finding out if this statement was true or not. For the millennium New Year I spent it in Las Vegas with a married couple from college, my brother Bud, and Kyle, a friend from high school. It was going to be a weekend of gambling, partying and fun…it was going to be non-stop. New Year's Eve day we started drinking at about 11 A.M., we thought we'd get the jump on the partying and figured it was the New Year somewhere in the world. We drank. We drank. And drank some more. We hit the strip. We gambled. We drank. You get the picture.

We went to the Strip and picked up some 32 oz. margaritas for the celebration, went back to the room and started playing drinking games.

Around 10 o'clock we decided to head back to the strip to hang out with the crowds…walk around and drink some more, if that was possible. By the time midnight rolled around the celebration was just beginning and I was ready for bed. It was kind of pathetic on my part, the biggest party night of the new millennium and all I wanted to do was go back to the hotel room and crawl into bed…and I actually wanted to go to bed alone. Not that I would have been able to hook up that night, my brother scared away all of the guys that I met on the strip. It was like I was 14 years old all over again. I started way too early and so did the couple we were with so I wasn't alone in my desire to sleep. The only people in the party mood were Bud, Kyle and about 10 thousand other people…so they weren't lonely without us party-poopers.

Before the night began, we figured out the sleeping arrangements…the married couple would of course get a bed, my brother Bud and I would get the other, and Kyle would get the cot. My brother would be safer than a friend from high school, known for his roaming hands. Around 4 A.M., Bud and Kyle came back to the room very very drunk, and woke all of us up from our somber sleep. I think they thought that if they were loud enough we might just wake up and join in on their fun. It didn't work, none of us were getting out of bed.

The drunk pair finally stumbled into their beds…I was relieved when my brother crawled into bed. I really just wasn't in the mood to fend off any unwanted moves. All I wanted to do was sleep. In less than five minutes I was nodding off, at this same time my brother began snuggling up to me like a date on prom night. I scooted over, thinking he was in a drunken state of confusion and I was just giving him the benefit of the doubt.

He snuggled up to me even more. I got scared. Then he began caressing my arm…I was horrified, just as you would have been too. I was freaking out, my mind was reeling, I didn't really know what to do but before he did anything that he'd regret, I hope, I had to put a stop to it, because if I scooted any further I would have fallen onto the floor. At that point I decided to "talk" to him…this is how it went:

> ME: *(getting up the courage)* "Bud, what are you doing?"
>
> *Silence…I was hoping that my loud initiation of conversation would put a stop to the madness.*

BUD: "Nothin'."

> *I was wrong, the madness didn't stop, and a moment or two went by when the moves began again.*

ME: *(screaming and squirming on the inside)* "Bud, I'm your sister!"

BUD: "So."

At that point, everyone in the room started laughing. Mine was a nervous laughter of course, but laughter nonetheless. That did the trick...after the humiliation and embarrassment, my brother decided to roll over and go to sleep...thank God. I don't know if I really slept that night, just in case Bud decided to give the old family fling another try. Luckily, the only other thing my brother decided to torture me with that night was his snoring.

Now that I have humiliated my brother, I feel like I have to explain. My brother has also tried to climb into bed with me and my boyfriend when I was in college...he was drunk then too. And, one Thanksgiving he tried climbing into bed NAKED with my mom and stepfather, oblivious to the fact that the bed was already full and, not to mention, full of family. We didn't let him live that one down for a really really long time...he's always good for a laugh or two if you get him drunk enough.

Funny drunk-ness runs in our family...along with the incest thing. Just kidding, I don't have that bad of taste. Incest is one thing that I will never ever ever attempt to experiment with, I can guarantee you that and I don't suggest that you give it a try either. YUCK. I'm just glad I survived my brush with incest unscathed, until the next time. Let that be a warning to you all, don't drink with relatives and if you do...lock your doors! Please lock your doors!

34

SODOMY ANYONE?

*A*nal sex. Ick, right? How could anyone do that? Exit only. It would hurt! There's no way *I'd* do that, let alone admit to it. Yeah right. I like anal sex, not all the time of course, but when the mood strikes there's nothing better.

I can remember the first time a guy wanted to do me in the ass…I was appalled; there was no way I was going to let him do THAT. At that point, I hadn't let anyone put ANYTHING up my rectum, not even a finger, nothing! But, of course, I eventually let him. You already know I'm incapable of saying no, there's nothing new there, but in this case I was drunk too. Eric was always good at convincing me into doing things, he was one of the first guys I gave a blowjob to and this was another first too.

The first time I had anal sex it did suck. For one, Eric didn't really know what he was doing. It hurt a little, and it didn't help that I was tense as hell. If you're going to do the backdoor tango, you've got to be relaxed otherwise there's no use in trying. It was a couple of years before I let a guy try it again, and a couple of more until I found a guy who knew what he was doing enough for me to really enjoy it. I'm very glad I gave it a real chance, otherwise I'd be missing out on all sorts of fun AND there's almost nothing better than an anal orgasm. You've got to give it a chance, seriously!

I know lots of women who would never do it. I know lots of women who have tried it, and don't like it. I know lots of women who do it, like it, but don't admit it. I admit that I have anal sex, and I admit that I like it when it's done right. It takes more finesse and control than regular sex...but can be oh so rewarding too. A lot of my girlfriends are so thankful that their men aren't interested in anal sex at all, but I guess those who don't like it have a way of finding each other. Just as those who do find someone who likes it too. I just don't understand how they won't even try it, they might actually like it...it's a wonderful thing.

It's not like I have anal sex with every guy I sleep with. I rarely initiate it; let's face it, there's really no elegant way of saying "will you fuck me in the ass?" I was sleeping with a forty year old man for almost a year before he made the anal sex move. I was shocked it took him so long...I was actually craving it. It was his loss because the "relationship" ended about a week later, and I know he wasn't getting that kind of action anywhere else. At about the same time, I was sleeping with a 22-year-old who mentioned that he'd never done it before, and I thought he was interested in giving it a try. But when I offered it up, he never acted on it. I think he was a little scared or freaked out about the whole thing. He probably had some homophobic worries or something juvenile like that...his loss and unfortunately mine too.

Other men out there seem to want it *too* much and are way too into it. Obsessed really. I don't want a guy who wants it every time...it would get boring and annoying, just like any technique that's been over-used. A little variety goes a long way.

A few suggestions: if you have any interest, try it once with someone you're comfortable with; do it face to face, it's better that way (trust me); and try throwing a toy into the mix after you get comfortable with the entire process. Oh and be safe about it too...STD and sanitarily speaking. If you need more info on the how to's there's a lot of info on the Internet...do a little research if you're not sure and enjoy!

35

BITE ME

*B*ITING! Don't do it!

Unless we ask. Unless it's just a nibble. Or a love bite. Otherwise, don't do it.

However, if we, and I mean me, moan in pleasure, please continue. If I scream, and I mean scream in pain, STOP! Don't do it again. It's not that difficult of a concept to understand, is it?

Those of you out there guilty of this and you know who you are, LEARN WHEN TO STOP.

A night of almost crazy passion left me with the bruise the size of a man's fist on my right arm, not like the bruise wasn't bad enough he had also left a welt to boot…adding insult to injury, I didn't even get laid. Roger was a biter; even though we'd slept together before, I didn't realize the extent of his need to bite, or at least his need to bite me. He generally left it at just biting my lower lip. The way he normally nibbled gave me the chills, but this wasn't like that at all.

On this particular night he was a little more aggressive than usual. At first

I didn't mind, I was enjoying the attention…and it didn't hurt at all that he was a beautiful male model. I'd almost let any man that looked like him "ravage" me a little, just not BITE, at least not hard.

The first time Roger bit me, and I mean BIT me, I screamed and screamed *loud*. I asked him what he was doing. He basically said he just wanted to eat me up alive, but he apologized. I just didn't think he literally wanted to eat me alive. I was hoping more for a figurative "eating." We fooled around a little until he did it again, fortunately for him we started drinking early on and by this time I was drunk, but it still hurt like hell and I told him to stop. Unfortunately, it was too late…the damage was done. The blood was already clotting in my arm, the moment was ruined, and the passion was gone. I was hurt, and I was temporarily physically and emotionally scarred.

It was so bad that my girlfriends thought I should take a picture and have him autograph it. It didn't go away for almost three weeks. When I'd go out without a long sleeve shirt I looked like I was the object of a little wife beating…and had the stares to prove it. In the future, I'm only going to ask nicely once, and that's it. If I have to ask twice you better protect the family jewels because I'll be looking to hurt you just like you hurt me. As the saying goes, "an eye for an eye," or in this case a "knee in the 'nads for a bite on the bicep."

Part VI

36

SUPER SIZE IT, PLEASE

The age-old question: If a tree falls in the forest and no one is there to hear it, does it make a sound? I don't know or care, but I have an answer to another age-old question: Does penis size matter to women? In a society of excess, penis size does matter! I have had the fortune to have many a big penis, but the misfortune to have encountered one too many small dicks too. I am not an expert and I'm sure that many women and men would disagree, but you'll have to trust me when I say, "YES definitely, size does matter...to me." Women hope that's not a banana in your pants, but you're just REAL happy to see us. Big penis, GOOD. Small penis, BAD. Average, OK (for those of you who don't know, I believe the national average is about five or six inches in length). I'm sorry guys, that's just the way it is...but there is hope, because there are exceptions to every rule and I break a lot of rules.

A one-night stand or a casual encounter is where size really does matter. The last thing you want is a mini-dog instead of a big old polish sausage when you're just there for sex—nothing more, nothing less. No romance. No emotion. No future. Don't waste adding a small cock to the list with a guy you barely know when there are so many other options out there. I mean, come on, you don't need a big one all the time; average does a pretty good job sometimes.

Unfortunately, it's kind of like a box of Cracker Jacks. You never know what the prize is until you open it. Sometimes you're happy with the do-dad you get, other times you get a lame old press-on tattoo of a skull and cross bones and you just feel screwed…and unfortunately that's the only way you'll feel screwed if you get a little penis. You win some and you lose some, but I really am a bad loser and I really really want to win—a lot. I'd much rather get the really cool prize, the really big dick, if I got to choose. I don't know any women who wouldn't.

I do believe, however, there is such a thing as a too big penis, once in awhile. A too big penis, although pretty to look at, can be uncomfortable. During sex it can hurt. While trying to give a blowjob, it can feel like you're choking or worse yet, feel like you're not getting the job done because you can't get more than 1/3 of it in your mouth. And forget about anal sex if it's too big. No way. Another downfall to the big dick syndrome is that a lot guys with big dicks don't know how to use their tool properly. They think that having the biggest unit on the block precludes them from having to be skillful at the task at hand. Well-endowed men seem to think that they can use their equipment like a battering ram: pure brute force and no finesses in their quest for an orgasm. Size alone is not enough. Apparently all those years of locker room comparisons and bragging rights went to their heads and they never learned that there are more important things to sex than just a big penis.

I admit that a big penis does often lead to good sex, a lot, but the last big dick man I slept with was the worst at oral sex or any foreplay for that matter. The sex was good, but the overall experience was very disappointing. It seems that this is a common aliment in well-endowed men. What if women with large breasts were almost always awful at blowjobs or bad in bed? Men would throw up their arms in protest, refusing to let us get away with it. It's that old double standard at work …guys with big dicks get the best of both worlds. Big Penis, laziness in bed. What more could a man want? Fortunately, for all you well-hung men, women boast of your manhood to anyone who will listen. When you're hung like a horse, expect the women to talk.

I've been very lucky in the size department. I had a boyfriend who had what I thought was an average-sized penis. It was about 7 inches. Darren was shocked when I told him I thought he was average, my average but average nonetheless. He'd never heard that from a girl before, since he was above the national average. He figured I'd had one too many extra big dicks, which skewed my perception of penis size! I'd have to agree, I have had a lot of big dicks…thank God!

There is a slight upside for women. Men with small to average penises are generally phenomenal at oral sex and other such techniques. They have to be great at pleasing a woman with their hands or tongues to compensate for their lack of size. Especially since every woman has had men who couldn't get the job done in the actual fucking department, they've had to resort to other means of finishing the job. I guess as long as they get the job done in one department or another that's all that matters to most girls. But I on the other hand want both—great sex and great foreplay. If they can't satisfy me in any area, they are doomed to not repeat. Because a girl just wants to be fucked good and hard once in awhile but also wants a man who knows his way around a vagina. Sex and orgasms are just way too important—to me and to everyone else with a healthy sex drive.

37

TEENY WIENIE

*I*tsy bitsy teeny wienie little…well, you get the picture. He's a small dick man. I think most men would prefer hearing the gasp of a satisfying "Ah!" or an "I've never seen one so big!" The last thing they want to hear when their Johnson's hanging out is "Oh, it's so cute." Although, I'm sure if they've heard it once, they've heard it twice…at least they had fair warning that they'd have to bone up on other skills besides fucking. Oh, the effort and determination of a slightly endowed man really is admirable. I wish all men tried so hard to please, but I guess some men don't have to try as much as their smaller counterparts, the poor things.

I have had more than one encounter with an undersized Johnson. I like to think that I dealt with each incident with style and hopefully a little grace, but I don't know if the ill-fated individuals thought so. For the average woman, there are only a couple of good things about a small penis. The first is that they don't make you gag when you're giving head; it's more like sucking a tootsie roll than some guy's dick, just not as tasty. Gagging really is the worst part about giving a blowjob; the average hummer is that much better on a small dick. Second, you don't really realize when they're inside you, which has happened more than once, unfortunately, but it normally means they're done before you know it…quick and painless, so you can get home and take a shower to wash the possible ick off and the memory of the little itty bitty thing too.

No matter what your size—big or small, fat or skinny—you must have confidence in it. Swing it like you just don't care. Swing it like it's a Louisville slugger and not a little league bat. If you don't have the confidence, we don't want to hear about it…it's the "don't ask, don't tell" penis policy. Unfortunately, not all men know this. Not all men know it's not wise to flaunt their paltry measure in front of us. For example, I was sleeping with a man who was so insecure that he did not measure up to average (he wanted 6 inches), he wanted to determine exactly what his size was. Tom was in his fifties and had never measured himself…I always thought that every guy did it at least once in high school or had a girl do it at some point, but not this guy.

Since all Tom wanted to do was measure up to average, he only needed to know whether or not he was six inches. At the time, we were in a hotel room with no ruler or measuring tape. He had to improvise because he was determined to know and know at that exact moment. Lucky or unlucky for him he knew that a dollar bill is exactly six inches long, providing the perfect rule of measure. At that point, Tom whips out a one-dollar bill, drops his pants to reveal a hard dick, and begins to measure…kind of, he didn't exactly know where to measure from. He was trying to cheat and gain an inch or so but after a little negotiating of the measurement, we determined that he did, just barely, measure up…to less than average. He was happy in his knowledge of his penis mediocrity and I did not have to bear any more rants of insecurity on his part. I, however, highly suggest that any other man or woman wanting to gage whether a penis is average or not use something other than a dollar bill, and if currency is a must, at least use a denomination greater than a dollar. If possible, use at least a Benjamin— that way you can use the large numbers to distract from the fact that the penis in hand may or may not be larger than six inches.

No matter how hard you try to avoid little dicks, sometimes experiencing one is not your fault nor is it of your choosing. Its not like boobs…it's pretty obvious when they're big or small. My friends will try and set me up with men they don't think are so bad…at least in their eyes. Luckily it's not that often, because they know I have weird taste too, but I'm beginning to believe that they have much worst taste than I. The last time my gay guy friends tried to set me up, it was with a guy they met in their gym. Supposedly, very hot and very nice. They checked him out in the shower and thought he met my minimal standards. Joe was a captain in the Air Force, stationed permanently outside of Los Angeles. Guys in uniform generally don't do it for me, but I had three guys tell me how "beautiful" he was, so I thought I'd give it a chance. I was between men so I really had nothing to lose.

I was given Joe's phone number to initiate the first call, to talk, get to know each other, and set up a time to meet. I called him on a Sunday night and he seemed nice. I mentioned that we should meet for coffee or drinks later in the week. He said he didn't want to meet until he knew I felt comfortable with the entire setup. It was coffee not sex! I didn't need to be comfortable, as long we weren't having drinks in a dark basement alone in the middle of nowhere. Public places are fine, but I agreed to get to know him a little over the phone...it couldn't hurt and the small talk on our first meeting would be minimal.

We talked the next night and things were good. It seemed like he had a decent personality and we had chemistry. I was attracted to him a little and we would talk for an hour or so at a time. I was getting to know him a lot, much more than if we would have met for drinks. We got to the point where Joe wanted to take me on a *real* date, which was kind of sweet. We talked every night for the next couple nights...we talked about all sorts of things, maybe things we shouldn't have talked about.

By Tuesday, we'd made plans for Friday night and by Wednesday night I was kind of getting sick of him. For one, Joe was starting to assume that we were going to sleep together when we met...I'm easy but I'm not a foregone conclusion, especially when I haven't even met the guy. And besides that, sleeping with me was the only thing he had any confidence about and I knew that wouldn't happen...at least not right away. You can't give in too quick to a guy who expects it. Joe was the most insecure guy I'd ever talked to. He was insecure about his looks, his career, and his personality. I don't know what my friends told him about me, but I think they gave me such a glowing description and raving reviews that it intimidated him. He was acting like he wasn't good enough for me, which he probably wasn't, but I didn't know that at the time.

During our enlightening conversations, Joe informed me that he had a small penis. A SMALL PENIS!!! I didn't want to know that...at least not yet. Old girlfriends had told him that he had a small penis and he checked out other guys' dick size in the gym for comparison too. Somehow he thought this information would be helpful to me in some way. I didn't need to know, at least not until it was up close and personal, especially before I met him or even knew what he looked like. I should have known though after he told me he was half Asian…it's a scientific fact that on average Asian males have smaller penises. He even mentioned the statistic…he might as well have worn a sign: "I'm Asian and have a small penis!" and saved himself the trouble of telling strangers.

If you have a small penis, we want it to be a surprise. After we know that there is chemistry and we're attracted to you, then we'll make the decision, right ladies? Don't just tell us out of the blue to warn us off…unless you don't want to have sex with us. You don't want to give us a lot of time to think about it because if we think about your penis being small and it potentially resulting in bad sex, we won't really want to do it with you. No matter how "cool" you are or how good of a time we had with you, it would make us hesitate and probably never want to do it…you'll stay in the friend zone. I never did go out with Joe. We had a dumb argument and never talked again. Oh well, I saved myself from sleeping with another small dick man who annoyed me.

I have to admit, however, I have had the unique pleasure of having some absolutely great sex with a small dick man. I was a freshman in college and it was my first real crush on campus. Stan was a freshman on the track team. He was cute. He was smart. We knew some of the same people and I knew he liked me too. I was young and completely infatuated and well, he could do no wrong. The first time we fooled around I was a little surprised by the lack of endowment. He had a great bod and wasn't insecure at all, so I just assumed. It was too late for me though, I liked him and, unfortunately, feelings always affect the "feeling" of a penis. No matter what Stan did, I loved it…the sex was incredible. I do believe that was the last time a small penis—and when I say small, I mean *small*—did the job well…very well. I'd even given him a second go around if I were to ever run into him again, to see if it was him or his penis that made the difference…so if you're out there, small penis man, look me up.

Since we're talking about penises, I really don't get the penis envy thing, I really don't…I mean I really love them, but I've never had penis envy in my life. The only way I would want my own is to play with but not have it as an actual body part. I do wish I had one to caress, pet, suck, fondle, and FUCK, but since I don't, thank God for technology. It's given me one of my own and it does things other penises can't...it vibrates at variable speeds and doesn't ever go soft and never gets jealous. Perfect!

I think big dicks are great to look at but it's weird when men talk about their penises. "My penis is beautiful!" "I have the perfect penis!", etc. What is that about? I've never heard a woman brag about how great her vagina is. Do men think that if they've got a prettier penis than the next guy, we'll fuck them instead? A lot of women don't even like looking at them. I, on the other hand, LOVE them, the way they look and feel, the way they react when you touch them, lick them, suck them.

In the end, I think I would just like to have a happy medium, a guy with a good-sized penis who knows how to use it, but also loves foreplay...it's not like I'm asking for a perfectly gorgeous man with a big bank book and a BIG cock. I just want the simple things in life, like every girl. Good, and frequent sex.

38

GETTING A HEAD

Blow jobs. BJ's. Smokin' the pole. Hummer. Giving head. Sucking the old tail pipe. The favorite foreplay move of people everywhere. Recently, a guy who works in the porn industry said the best blowjob ever given and recorded is in the movie CALIGULA, I would have to agree. Have you seen it? If you don't know what I'm talking about, go get the movie...on DVD if you can find it, it'll be worth your while.

Blowjobs are on everybody's mind...all the time it seems. It's the hot topic among women everywhere. I only like to give blowjobs to men I'm actually attracted to. If I'm not so attracted to you then I'd rather just fuck you...it's a lot less personal than having some random guy's cock in my mouth. Before I get into the blowjob thing too much, I have to say that hygiene and hair make a huge difference. A man has to be clean...from head to toe. This is the most important factor in whether or not a guy is going to get head from a girl. I would say an unshaved, untrimmed, and unclean penis is the worst...really, how hard is it to shower every day and do a little lawn mowing once in awhile? Do yourself a favor, everyone, be clean...we like that, and if we don't, we're just weird.

I like it when a man trims, even shaves a little, but a man who only leaves a "beard" or any other small patch of hair takes a lot getting used too. Unless you have hair issues like one of my girlfriends, she likes her men shaved from neck to toes. But, it's only fair. I shave, leaving only a landing strip usually…it's like anything else, I change it when the mood strikes. I also keep it nice and trim for the man I'm with and they should do the same. I floss regularly on my own; I don't need pubic-flavored floss to finish the job nor do I need to cough up a hairball once a month to add to the experience. If you're not comfortable shaving or trimming yourself, get your girl to do it for you. Unless she likes going through the jungle to get to the tree, she'll appreciate you wanting to cut it all down. Ladies, if your man needs some hygiene lessons do it nice, maybe in the shower and finish the lesson off with a BJ. Trust me he'll get the hint.

A "straight" guy recently told me that he wasn't going to give any blowjobs to get ahead in the entertainment business, which I was relieved to hear since I was sleeping with him. I told him that I'd obviously been blowing all of the wrong people, considering I'm just a glorified secretary working for really insane assholes in the entertainment business. But I like to give blowjobs and that's the key to doing anything well, enjoying it. If you don't enjoy it, don't do it…there nothing worse than a man who doesn't like to eat me out—especially if he's bad at it or won't do it at all. I guess it's probably the same for men when they hookup with a woman who doesn't like giving oral. The men in my life, however, never have that problem because I wouldn't stand for it very long. They'd be out the door faster than usual, but I'd be the one kicking them out.

I know a lot of girls say they give a good or—even great—BJ, but don't actually know how to follow through with their claim. Those girls leave the target of their hard effort and resulting lockjaw unsatisfied in their great orgasmic quest. But I, however, can make that claim. Normally, I wouldn't brag too much about giving BJs, but in this venue I have a right too. Unfortunately, now that I've made this claim, I'll probably be giving a lot less, just because I've now set my own personal standard and performance expectation so high. But in a relationship or a one-night stand, it's about give and take and if I get, I'll give no matter the expectation. If a guy isn't going to eat me out often, there's no way in hell I'm going to be doing it very often for him, unless I'm *really* in the mood. I don't really get chicks that don't like doing it. There's power and control when you go down on a guy…it's the only natural power position a woman has during sex. There's more control than at any other time, unless you've got the guy tied to a bed or if your man's into being dominated, but that's beside the point. Bottom line, I like it and it gives me power, but no matter how it makes me feel, I gotta get some in return.

It's definitely been a long road to getting good at it and even enjoying it. I think that part of the enjoyment process is that I know I'm pretty damn good at it…some say the BEST. Nine out of ten users agree! If you want references I can give you those too. A lot of people enjoy things much more when they know they're doing a good job and their work is really being appreciated, and I know I'm appreciated. That's the thing, most women don't understand that men will appreciate the effort. They don't care how you do it, as long as you don't bite. Of course they'll like it a lot more if you do it well, but they won't stop you from sucking them off even if you have poor technique…it just might take longer.

I've taught more than one of my girlfriends how to give a better blowjob. I recommended that my last "student" rent some good blowjob porn…if you're going to learn, learn from the pros. She wasn't too keen on the porn idea. I don't think she'd ever watched porn, let alone gone to the video store, gone behind the curtain, and picked out a good one to rent. I then mentioned that she could take a class I had heard about. A woman, author and lecturer in Beverly Hills named Lou Paget teaches housewives and such how to give a good and proper blowjob. The class is fairly expensive, but you can take it with a group of people…it's like a Tupperware party, refreshments and everything, but instead of buying something to keep your leftovers in, you're buying something that will help you keep your man fresh and hopefully monogamous. A bunch of coifed stuck-up women sitting in a Bel-Air living room practicing giving oral pleasure on a banana: I'd love to be a fly on the wall for that class.

While I was an assistant for one of my prudish female bosses, I found a handout and her notes from the Lou Paget class. It was hilarious, but I wasn't surprised. She was a trust fund baby and was probably raised thinking that having a guy's dick in her mouth was disgusting. I was really glad to see that she was willing to get down and dirty. She'd have to learn to keep a man happy; money isn't everything and that's all she had—no personality, no class. While I was perusing the outlined handout I even learned a thing or two. I'm all about honing my craft because you CAN teach an old dog a new trick or two once in awhile.

I digress. Back to the story at hand. With no banana handy or any other comparable fruit on hand, I resorted to using a ballpoint pen to teach my inept friend. It was the only phallic-looking instrument around to illustrate a basic technique that would work for her. She was mortified, but I thought it hilarious. I went to town, figuratively of course, on the pen attempting to show her the basic tricks of the trade. She generally would go down for a maximum time of about three minutes...which is better than nothing, but I encouraged her to stay a little longer on her guy's Johnson. On top of this, she didn't know it was a good thing to use her hands in conjunction with her mouth. Stuff I thought was common sense was completely foreign to her. She reported a few days later that it went pretty well and that her man was very happy with the improvements. My good sexual deed for the day was done...another decent blowjob was delivered with great satisfaction.

I thought my teaching days were over because now all the girls I know give great blowjobs. But recently my friend Don, who is pushing 40, started dating a 21-year old virgin...he happily fixed the first obstacle, de-virginizing her, the first chance he got. But the second was getting her to do all of the things he wanted her to do in bed: giving head, accepting oral sex, etc. First and foremost on his mind was getting her to give him a good—actually great—blowjob. Without asking her first, he requested that I teach her how to give a proper BJ. I was flattered and would happily teach her a few tricks...spread the knowledge, spread the fun.

Now, I've never given Don a hummer, but he assumed that I knew what I was doing...well, not exactly assumed, I told him that I was great and I had a couple of references he knew of to prove it. First, I told him that the best way for a girl to learn is to have the man she's with instruct her based on what he likes...his exact quote was "It's been a long, long time since I've had a good one so I can't remember what's involved." I laughed my ass off and then agreed to teach her, but only if she agreed to it. I'm still waiting for her call...I guess her supposed extreme shyness and the thought of a total stranger teaching her how to give a banana pleasure just wasn't her cup of tea. Don will just have to keep searching for the ultimate blowjob.

As long as you're eager and willing you can learn to do anything well, or at least good enough. If you're a guy and having a hard time getting the girl you're with to give you a blowjob or give it well, let her know how much it turns you on, encourage her. It's like anything else, compliments will get you everything…especially in bed. Even if I'm not the best head a guy's gotten, compliments make me feel good, they make me want to do it even more, do better, top the last orgasm. Simple isn't it? I can't wait until I give another blowjob…who's next?

39

THE HARD WAY

I don't think it's really fair that I had to learn how to give blowjobs through trial and error, the real hard way…pun intended. There wasn't anyone like me around to teach me the ropes. I started giving blowjobs about the same time I started having sex, which was a really really long time ago. At first I was just putting the guy's penis in my mouth and going up and down—pretty boring and basic really. At the time, I guess it was good enough for adolescents. High school boys are just happy to have about anyone's mouth on their dick, especially someone who's eager to please.

Along the way, I did have a couple of guys who were very vocal about what they wanted, giving me good directions that I always remembered and used. I don't necessarily think I'm that great at sex, but I think I'm pretty good at the other stuff. It's the confidence that's important; in all the things in life, you want to do well. Either that or it's just because I've been doing it for so long, learning from my mistakes, and doing it over and over and over. It really is true what they say: practice makes perfect.

Like anyone just starting out, I fought the gagging…still do sometimes if a man is too big, but I actually try to avoid the really big ones for blowjobs, just in case the gagging isn't under control. I've had one too many bad experiences while giving a big dick man a BJ. When I was in high school I was seeing this older guy, Josh, from another town, we'd get drunk and fool around in the back of his pickup...I can't believe I've actually fooled around more than once in the back of some guys dirty truck. God, I hope I never have to go that route ever again in my sexual life...I much prefer the Four Seasons to Ford.

No matter the location, it was always hot. I always wanted to fuck Josh, but for some reason or another we didn't. I think partially because he never actually made the "sex move" but also because he had a girlfriend (although that didn't stop us from hooking up every week and doing everything except intercourse). It was a lot of fun, generally. Once when we were both drunk I was giving him a blowjob and, since I was still learning the ropes, I couldn't quite control my weak gag reflexes. I threw up all over Josh, while he was in my mouth. It was disgusting and I was humiliated. Thankfully, he didn't seem to mind too much; he just grabbed a beer and washed himself off like it happened to him all the time...which it probably did. I even finished the task at hand, even though I was miserable, but Josh was such a good sport, I had too.

Apparently, I'm not the only one of my peers this has happened to—I asked around, a lot. From then on I knew not to give head drunk and on a full stomach, at least not until I mastered the technique, and to avoid the big prick if I could. Since then I've gotten a little better, because I've learned a few more moves in the last couple years that have helped me out. Fewer do's than don't in the tips department, but it's all the same in getting better at what you love.

Scott, one of my guy friends, recently asked me how to get a girl to give him head. He says he has no problem getting a girl to sleep with him, but getting her to suck the pole is a whole different ball game. It didn't surprise me that Scott found himself in this predicament; some women find that it's easier to just let a guy fuck them...less effort and, for some, less personal. When I'm not completely attracted to a guy and just want to get the sex over with I'll pursue intercourse with no foreplay. I don't just put any dick in my mouth...I have some standards.

I told Scott that if a girl wants to do it she's going to do it, plain and simple. We don't necessarily like it when you push our heads down to get us to give you a blowjob. The head-pushing thing is just plain stupid on a guy's part, even if we were planning on doing it that could cause us to change our minds. We don't like being told either…well, unless we like being dominated, but that's another issue. However, I think that if you express your desire for one and you have a giving partner, they'll do about anything…but that's just my opinion. Generally, most women will reciprocate if you do a good job for her. If you don't give oral sex, don't expect to get any yourself.

Scott has decided that his next line will be that he's never had a good blow job before, because I told him a man said that to me once and a blowjob was the first thing I did. I knew it was a line, but it worked nonetheless. It's my secret weapon and I had to unleash the big arsenal on a man who so adamantly denied wanting and enjoying a blowjob. I think he's now spoiled and has even a harder time enjoying the average BJ. Once you've had the best, how can you be content with anything else? The bottom line: I'm good at it and I enjoy it.

40

CURIOUSLY STRONG

I'm sure most of you out there have tried some kind of stimulant to enhance giving or receiving head. Which means you've probably tried the Altoids technique, right? Or something similar? Well, if you haven't, it's basically putting Altoids or anything else with a cooling effect in your mouth while giving head. It gives the penis a tingly, cold sensation and it makes it taste fresh and minty as well. The thing is, I never felt a need to enhance or alter my performance in that way, at least not until I dated a guy who liked to experiment and I thought I'd just give it a try, it couldn't hurt right?

We had a great sex life, but I wanted to make it better, give Barry something to talk to his friends about. So, one day I was prepared...I had a tin of Altoids by the bed and was craving a penis in my mouth. When he was about to get out of the shower, I decided I would surprise Barry with the new technique, something I know he'd never had before and I thought he would love. I popped the Altoids in my mouth, letting them soak in and begin to work, and waited anxiously for him to come out of the bathroom.

When Barry came out, I threw him on the bed and went to town, not giving him one second to stop me or question what I was doing. Initially, he was more than excited, but soon I realized something was wrong. Very wrong. He was going soft while he was in my mouth, and this had never happened before. Barry would get hard, and then soft, then hard, but he was fast becoming as limp as a dead fish. He didn't say anything, so I continued to try my best to regain the excitement I had lost. I was doing everything right, or so I thought, but it didn't matter, nothing was working.

I decided to take this opportunity to ask him if there was something wrong. Barry said, with confusion, that it was "cold," damn COLD. I said that it was supposed to be a little chilling, but in a good way. At that point I couldn't really figure out what was wrong. I tried everything to no avail. Barry said that since it was supposed to be a "good" thing, he'd let me try again, but reluctantly.

After I gave up, what seemed like hours later, Barry was no longer in the mood to fool around so we started to talk about the experience. He asked what it was that made his dick so cold. I told him it was Altoids. He then asked why I would do that to him—put Altoids in my mouth? I told Barry that all my friends had said it was a great thing to do while giving a blowjob. I then asked him why he didn't like it…Barry said it was like his dick was being "frozen off." I told him I was sorry, after I stopped laughing of course and that I didn't know it was going to do that. Barry begged and pleaded with me to never try it again. I agreed but was disappointed, it had killed the mood and all he wanted to do at that point was smoke a cigarette and take a nap.

Later, while on the way to the movies with a friend, Amber, I told her that I had tried the Altoid thing, because I was still a little confused. I wanted to know if it was just my man who didn't like it or if I was doing something wrong. I told her he didn't like it and that he thought it was too cold. Amber thought this was weird and asked me what *exactly* did I do. I told her that while he was in the shower I put five Altoids in my mouth. Amber shouted "FIVE?" And almost drove us off the road. She was laughing so hard we almost got in a wreck. Apparently five is three or four too many.

I like to experiment but I learned my lesson, the penis is a very sensitive organ, and if you put too many Altoids, or anything else too cold, in your mouth before you give a blowjob, it'll "freeze their dick off"…which is not a good thing if you want to get any action afterwards. I haven't actually attempted giving head again with Altoids, but I know that when I do, I'll do it right...only one or two at a time. I wonder who the lucky fellow, I mean victim will be. Volunteers anyone?

41

THE SPREAD-ABLE DELIGHT

Have you ever had Nutella? It's a delicious hazelnut spread. I tried it recently, kind of a 29th birthday present to myself. The opportunity arose and I took it fully and eagerly. It's just something I had never thought about trying before, but I'm sure glad that I finally did. It had just never been presented to me properly—everybody knows it's all in the presentation.

Jose, a very hot Hispanic man I worked with, introduced me to the delicious spread. It happened one night after an unsettling discussion with one of my recent ex-boyfriends. I had spoken to Jose on the phone and he noticed that I was upset. He asked me to come over to watch a movie, just as friends. We'd never hooked up before but we flirted like mad and I had hoped that something would eventually happen between us because he was just so beautiful. I just didn't think it would be that night. Naively, I thought he really did just want to be my friend and wanted to watch a movie with me.

Lucky for me, the minute I walked into his house, he was all over me. He threw me onto his lap, to comfort me in my momentary sadness regarding my ex. I knew immediately he didn't want to just be my friend by the pole in his pants. I protested the advances for a moment, while enjoying the bulge. I really didn't think it was a good idea because my mind was somewhere else that night. I was afraid, however, that there might not be another opportunity so I couldn't say no—especially not to someone with an incredible body like Jose's.

He had just come home from working out and he was all sweaty, he mentioned we should take a "friend" shower together. After watching him undress in the candlelight, I jumped at the chance at getting clean with him…or dirty as I really hoped. It was the best shower scene I've ever had and it didn't stop there. I didn't know the positions we achieved were possible in a shower, but I haven't been able achieve them since, either. We went at it for hours and hours…thank God.

From the shower, where we had incredible sex, he conned me into giving a back massage, which I eagerly gave, as an excuse to touch him from head to toe. We had sex literally every which way we could. Front, back and side-to-side, in the shower, on the couch, in the bedroom, in the kitchen. He was unbelievable and I was just enjoying every moment.

We took a break from the marathon sex session and Jose, naked, went to the kitchen so I followed. He had the munchies. He was eating Nutella out of the jar. He asked if I wanted any and of course I said yes, I was starving; we'd worked up quite an appetite. I went to take the spoon from him, but he wouldn't give it to me. He took the spoon with the Nutella and placed it on his perfectly curved penis. If I wanted to try any, I had to try it *his* way; I liked his way much better than a boring old spoon. It was the best method for trying a new spread-able delight. It was so delicious I went back for seconds, and even thirds.

After our snack, we went for another round of play. Overall it was quite memorable and, ever since, I do try to integrate food or other flavorful things into sex and foreplay…it's much more fun and a girl's got to eat, doesn't she? You've got to give it a try, really you do! I highly recommend it whether it's Nutella, Hershey's syrup, or any other yummy thing you can eat off of your lover. What better reason to ruin a diet?

Part VII

42

JUST SAY NO...MAYBE

I t's hard to say no—at least when it comes to sex and men. It really is and if you don't already know it, you'll just have to trust me. I've actually said "no" a few times. I haven't said it much since my sexual activities began. I can probably count on two hands, or maybe even one, the times I've actually said "no" as an adult. Instead of "No," I just avoid those situations. I really should take one of those assertiveness seminars that teach people how to say "no" to family, salesman, and such...I would then try to learn how to say "NO" to men and sex. It's an art form I obviously haven't mastered.

In high school, I didn't know how to say it. "No" was like a foreign language or a bad word. They should teach that along with how to bake a pie or how to tie your shoes. You know how many mistakes I could have avoided by knowing how to say that two letter word? But you see, I don't know if I ever wanted to say it. I thought that's how you got a guy to like you. No matter the guy, no matter the situation.

I envy those who can say "no." "No" to dates. "No" to sex. "No" to anything you really don't want to do passionately. I have a problem with boundaries obviously, but it's something else I'm working on. There should be a campaign promoting saying "no," not just to drugs, not to just sex, but for saying "no" to bad sex. I'd buy that t-shirt "Just say 'No' to bad sex!" If I had the ability to say "no" to bad sex, then my list would be cut down by at least a third.

Oddly enough, I've found I can sometimes easily say "no" to some guy who expects to have sex with me. Why is that? It's probably the part of me that doesn't like to be told what to do. Or that, once in awhile, I like being a challenge or a bitch, probably the latter of the two. I have even found myself saying "no" to some guys I've already had sex with. I'm not really sure what that's all about, but normally I just give in, mostly because I can't remember why I was saying "no" to begin with. It's not like they haven't made The List. And repeats are the best people to have "random" sex with. Your needs are being met, but you're not adding to your numbers...if that matters.

Wanting to be easy and not a total "slut" going out and having unsafe one-night stands, I have found that is the best way to have my sexual needs met. However, at times fucking repeats can be boring. What's the point of going back to the trough when you've already eaten there unless it was a gourmet meal to begin with? Then I'd be in line for seconds all the time.

I'm so bad at saying "no" that it is a problem in every aspect of my social life. When friends ask for a favor, I generally say yes, even if I don't want to do it. Or when a boss asks me to work on a Saturday and I already have plans. Or when a guy asks for my number it's hard for me to say "no." In situations pertaining to the opposite sex, if I feel like I'm going to be put in a situation where I might want to say "no," I try to avoid it altogether. That doesn't always work, obviously, since you can't predict when a sexual situation will arise. When those circumstances come up, through trial and error, I have gotten fairly good at figuring out ways to avoid actually saying "no." Particularly when it might hurt someone's feelings or I don't feel that's it's worth the effort of actually saying "no." I know I'm chicken, I'm telling you again, I'm a chicken. I'm OK with that, I really am. It is yet another problem I'm working on in therapy.

My best weapon for my defense has been something that has been around for decades. The telephone. I've always believed that you must make the phone company work for you. Even though, if I could live my life without one I would. I know no one is forcing me to answer the phone when it rings, but at times it's so unavoidable. I do have caller I.D. with blocked number rejection, so I know when my friends are calling, but you never know who might call you unexpectedly…besides those annoying telemarketers.

One day in traffic on Olympic Boulevard, a guy in an SUV kept trying to get my attention. I ignored him at first, but he was kind of cute and since we were stuck in traffic next to each other I couldn't disregard him for long. I rolled down my window and he introduced himself. He seemed nice and I wasn't seeing anyone at the moment so I decided to give him a chance…something I know I need to stop doing—giving random guys my real number.

It didn't take long until Zach called; we actually spoke on the phone a few times. Supposedly he was a busy stockbroker, so we didn't make plans to meet in person right away. I soon got bored of him, especially after he said he'd "make time in his schedule to see me" with no regard to my own calendar. I tried nicely to get Zach to stop calling, but I didn't do it very well and he continued to call. I'm not very good at dropping hints or being indirect either, which is a very bad thing when you're too chicken to reject anyone outright.

Thankfully, Zach called from the same two numbers every time. I, being the phone freak that I am, had select call forwarding on my phone. I decided if I couldn't say "no" and I couldn't get rid of him the "nice way," I would forward his two numbers to a disconnected number. Every time Zach would try calling he would get the "this number is no longer in service" message. Rejection accomplished!

I know, I'm a wimp. Select call forwarding may not have been created for that purpose, but I'm resourceful and know how to use my surroundings as my best defense…and at least I didn't lead Zach on, right? Right? I can't be the only backbone-less creature out there with the need of a chastity belt and a dose of courage, but I figure that's the least of my problems. I do try. Really I do. I mean, I've said "no" occasionally but only on the occasions where the man is absolutely annoying and not worth even the effort to have sex with…it's got to be pretty bad if I don't say yes.

43

PITY SEX AT THE MOTEL SIX

Have you ever had sex with someone that you really don't want to do it with? Have you ever felt so sorry for a guy or girl that you just decided to make their day and fuck the shit out of them? Or lie there like a wet blanket and let them fuck you? Sometimes if a man has put in his time, done his duty, and is just really pathetic and gives off the impression that he hasn't been laid in years, sometimes you have to throw a dog a bone. Sometimes it's easier just to do it than to make the effort to say no, especially if it's someone you don't plan to see again…EVER.

Someone on my List comes to mind immediately as a Pity Fuck. Cain was, well in one word, annoying. In two words, small dick. I must say he did entertain me and put in the time for about a week before I decided I needed to put out. I was bored and felt a little guilty, I don't like to lead guys on and I probably led him on a little bit, so of course I had sex with him.

The only flaw to this plan is that normally these guys never get laid so they think if you give it up once you'd give it up again. Not true, especially if it's bad to begin with. I do everything in my power, after the fact of course, to discourage any future outings…in a roundabout way of course. No confrontation. No "No." Just a gentle, "Oh, I'm busy, but thanks." Pathetic, I know…but it's me we're talking about. Not only can I not say "no," but I can't even say, "Hey can you at least take me to a nice hotel?" I can't get a man to take me to a Holiday Inn. Instead I get the oh-so-luxurious Motel 6. Why is that? It's because I have BAD TASTE of course. I sure do know how to pick them, don't I? Cheap fucking bastards.

Not only did I have sex in a Motel 6 with Cain, but it was really bad pity sex. I guess that's what I get for having such low expectations. It was so bad that once it started, it was over…it ended so quickly that I barely felt it…oh wait, that was the only good thing about the experience. That's something to say about a man with a small penis, you don't feel it. I just couldn't get out of there fast enough and Cain actually thought he'd get seconds. ICK! Yeah right! And increase my chances of getting more kooties. Maybe at a Hyatt, but definitely not at a Motel 6.

Luckily, I didn't have to stay the night. Too bad Motel 6 doesn't rent by the hour. Cain could have saved almost all of that $36 he had to fork out for a little Saturday night romp. A friend of mine, Leeza, got some one-night stand hotel sex recently and she complained that he had the hotel scoped out and the money ready. I asked Leeza what she was complaining about? He spent $150 on the room and in a nice hotel with a view! It was much better than the Motel 6 I had sex in…the uncomfortable bed, the cheap surroundings, etc. I told Liza she should feel flattered, he definitely didn't think she was a cheap whore, just a $150 a night whore…she's not a whore but there's nothing to be ashamed of either. I would have gladly changed places with her, especially since she gave him a thumbs-up in the performance area.

I wish that was my only pity-sex story, but it's not. Now that I think about it, there have been many…too many. Another that comes to mind is when I was in the 3rd grade. A boy in my class, Todd, had a huge crush on me. I remember he would come to school with little presents for me, like jewelry (fake of course, he was only in the 3rd grade for God's sake) and other stuff he made. It was very sweet. And I know what you're probably thinking and NO I did not sleep with him then…gross, we were like eight years old.

Todd moved away a couple of years later and I didn't see him again until I was in college. We met up for drinks one night and I soon discovered he still had a crush on me. I had to make his "dream" come true, so I had sex with him. Even though the years did not create an attraction to him, I just couldn't break his heart again. We never saw each other after that...which was definitely for the best, at least for me.

It's the least I can do, right? Have sex with a guy who probably hasn't had any sex, at least free sex, in months, if not years. And that's just two of the stories...but it made me wonder how many pity fucks *I've* been given? I'm playing it safe and telling myself NONE, at least none yet. Someday, I do realize that I may be in the need of a pity fuck or two in my future...I figure the more pity fucks I give, the more I might get in return for all my humanity! So, ladies and gentlemen, don't be afraid to give it up a little because you never know when you'll need a little pity yourself!

44

TIGHTIE-WHITIES

*E*very once in awhile I'll say NO purely based on principle. It's rare, but it happens. Principle is very important to me…even if my principles are a little out of whack. These principles have kept me out of a couple beds I had no business being in. So, I guess I have to be thankful I have some minimum standards for sleeping with a man. I was beginning to think that I had no standards at all. I guess I can't give it up to just anyone.

I met a guy, Matt, at my dry cleaners one night. He seemed nice and asked for my number. He called and we decided to meet for drinks in Beverly Hills. He was late, I was early so I started drinking without him, then more when he got there. I got loaded drinking Mojitos…it's a drink with mint, rum, sugar and club soda and it's lethal—very strong and very sugary. After about three or four of them, we went to his place for another drink. That was the first mistake, well actually, probably the second. The first was getting loaded to begin with, but in my defense those drinks were just heavenly and I'd probably do it again too.

Anyway, Matt was making us more drinks; he was obviously more than happy to get me even more plastered. Keeping myself busy, I showed myself around, and immediately I was awed by his unintentionally decorated disco apartment. It had mirrored walls and old 70's furniture. I'm sure Matt thought it was the ultimate bachelor's pad, but it really was a turn-off...especially for a man in his late thirties. When I landed in the bedroom, which didn't take long since it was a one-bedroom apartment, I noticed the leopard pattern comforter and satin sheets. I should have listened to my instincts and ran away right then, but I didn't. I stuck around to get molested by a guy who apparently thinks that the best time to make a move on a girl is while she's throwing her guts up in the bathroom. I mean who wouldn't be turned on by that? I know I would—if I liked girls and vomit.

The fun didn't stop there. I woke up the next day, completely hung over and dressed only in his t-shirt...he, only in his tightie-whities. I vaguely remembered him trying to put the moves on while undressing me completely. I, luckily, wasn't so out of it that I couldn't keep him off me. He just got a cheap thrill I guess...which is more than I got, that's for sure.

For some reason...bad taste...I decided to go out with Matt again. This time I wouldn't drink. We went to a Lakers game, then back to the bachelor pad. We fooled around a little bit but just to second base. I guess there is a little prude in me somewhere. When it got right down to it, I just couldn't bring myself to sleep with a guy who wore tightie-whities and owned leopard print bedding. A girl can't help what turns her off. I made up some excuse to leave and got out of there quick.

Matt called a few days later to see if I wanted to go out again. I had to give the guy credit for continuing to try with me. Especially since the furthest he got was on the first date and it just went downhill from there. I just had to be honest, he deserved that, I told Matt that the tightie-whities had to go, and not onto the floor in a crumpled mess. I told him I just couldn't have sex with a 36-year-old man who still wore Fruit of the Looms.

We went out one more time but Matt told me he wouldn't change his well-chosen wardrobe for me...not even to have sex. I never did sleep with him and all he had to do was buy a pair of boxers, that's it! A man probably wouldn't really find me too attractive if all I wore were granny-panties...he'd probably get over it faster than I by just ripping them off me, but I just had to stand by my principles. You'd do the same thing too, right? Particularly if you were looking for a good excuse to not sleep with a man.

45

THE LEG HUMPER

Have you watched those nature shows on the Discovery Channel? You know the ones with the mating rituals of animals and insects. Lions and bears and squirrels and beetles, oh my… mating…going at it, well, going at it like animals. Has your leg ever been attacked by a horny dog…man or animal? Or have you watched someone be molested by a wayward pooch looking for an easy lay? Count your blessings if you've never had a first-hand experience with a dog dry humping your leg…I can tell you, it is NOT pleasant.

I have had the misfortune of a dog dry-hump me…well, not a canine exactly, but a human male dog. A grown man tried to hump my leg. Don't get me wrong, I'm not against a little making out followed by a lot of rubbing and bumping and grinding. Massaging and stroking at times can be an unexpected and more enjoyable way to reach your climactic goal than sex, mostly because it doesn't happen for me too often post high school days. I figure, if you're going to fool around, you might as well just do it, but if you don't want to have sex with a man, I guess dry humping is as good of an out as any.

My "dog," Perry, was an ex-European pro soccer player. He had a great body and he was cute enough I guess, not really my type though but cute enough to fool around with. I was bored and looking for a good distraction. I had been involved with a man who had a girlfriend and I desperately wanted to find a replacement. Any replacement! I wanted to be ravaged but I soon realized I didn't want to be ravaged by just anyone...just by my "taken" man. I was screwed and not the way I wanted to be.

Perry was a manager at a restaurant near my office. I was walking by one day and he made a move on me. That's the good thing about Europeans—they're not afraid of pretty girls. Being the idiot dater that I am, I didn't even know I was being hit on even after he asked for my number. I thought it was for some restaurant promotion or something. It wasn't until he called me that night that I got clued in. We spoke for a little bit, then Perry asked me if I wanted him to bring over a bottle of wine. I, for some stupid reason, thought this was a good idea. That was my first mistake, or second...I've lost count.

The minute Perry arrived, I knew it was a bad idea. He was insanely aggressive. I initially thought it was the foreigner in him, but he was even more aggressive than the average European I'd dated. While we sat on the couch, I used my glass of wine like it was a chastity belt, blocking Perry at his every move, not wanting him to come any closer. At about this time I wondered, again, why I allowed him into my home and why I just didn't throw him out. Perry's persistence finally wore me down, so I let him kiss me a little bit. I knew instantly, as we women sometimes do, that it wouldn't go very far. Mostly because he was such a bad kisser, but also there wasn't much chemistry. Still somehow, someway, we ended up in my bedroom. I have blocked that part out of my mind because I'm still perplexed by how he got us in there. Maybe he hypnotized me or tricked me or just plain asked me, but I just can't figure out how it really happened.

I watched Perry take off his pants, perplexed *again* by this move, since we'd barely kissed at that point. The voice in my head was me asking myself why he was taking his pants off. I hate it when a guy assumes he's going to get some, especially when I had no plans on sleeping with him in the first place. But there I was with a half-naked European in my bed. Perry was all over me and it was one of the few times in my life that I just laid there like a wet blanket, waiting for him to make his next move, hoping I wouldn't have to kick him in his European soccer nuts and force him off of me.

It was then I realized that Perry was trying to get me excited by his performance of HUMPING MY LEG! I was still fully clothed at the time and I was in complete shock. I really didn't know what to do. It's not like he was rubbing up against anything that was making me feel good…my right thigh is not generally considered an erogenous zone. He could have gotten some if he would have focused on me for more than three seconds. Instead he was, well, humping my leg. AND I was not enjoying it. Not at all!

I was getting bored and just wanted him to finish whatever he was attempting to do. I don't know how long I lay their letting Perry use me like an abused pillow, when he finally stopped. At this point, he knew he wasn't really getting anywhere with me.

I let Perry leave without walking him to the door because I couldn't get rid of him fast enough. I was glad to have him out of my house and off my leg. Then I realized Perry had finished his task and left a little proof behind…a big old wet spot on my pants. Yuck! Exactly where he was attempting to bump and grind me. He came. He came on me—through his briefs and onto me. I was mortified. Not only did Perry hump me like a dog in heat, he stained my favorite pants. I guess I deserved it, for being the easy idiot that I am and letting a complete stranger into my house. I'm lucky I only got a little stain and not something much more horrible.

Unfortunately, the joy of Perry didn't stop there. I kept running into him because we worked near each other and he kept asking me out. On one of those occasions I made a reference to the gift he left behind. Perry denied having an orgasm, which was even scarier since I didn't think there was any way it was pre-cum. Then I started to think he'd peed on me, which really freaked me out even more, as if that was possible. The poor guy, someone should tell him humping a girl's leg is no way to get laid. However, to illustrate my bad taste, yet again, I went out with Perry again. Thankfully, I didn't even allow him to first base and there was no repeat performance of the leg humping. I was spared.

Since this experience I have developed the "Emergency Guide to Avoid the Wayward Leg Humper." You never know what skills you'll need to have in order to get out of such an awful position.

The Emergency Guide:

1. Be a responsible citizen, spay or neuter your *dog*! Avoid potential exposure to canine horniness.

2. Don't be an idiot and let a *dog* into your home or personal space—you're asking for trouble. If you do, check for fleas or any other contagious elements before making contact.

3. Know where to scratch your *dog* in just the right place to get that leg-humping action off of you and in the appropriate place, wherever that may be.

4. Keep *dog* biscuits or other such treats around to distract your *dog* just long enough to escape...I suggest keeping porn in your purse at all times, preferably with some girl-on-girl action, it'll give you that 15 second window of opportunity to get the hell out of there.

5. Contact your local humane society when all else fails...that's what they're there for: to rescue you from the unwanted mutt.

I know it's not a great emergency guide, but what did you expect? I obviously can't get myself out of these kinds of situations gracefully or at all for that matter. I'm still working on the simple task of saying "no!" But I do genuinely wish you "Good Luck!" and I hope no wayward *dog* humps you anytime soon...unless you really like that sort of thing.

46

HANDY MAN

At times, when I don't feel like having sex or giving a guy a blowjob and it's already gone too far to say no without being a tease, and instead of adding them to The List or pity fucking them, I'll give them a hand job or let them do the job for themselves in my presence. Sweet isn't it? There's nothing wrong with it either, if that's what you're thinking. They're getting what they want and the end justifies the means, even if it is a little messier in the end and not quite as personal… and hand jobs are the new "it" thing, didn't you know?

I was sleeping with Nate for over six months when I decided to end it. Nate knew that the end was coming, but was surprised by the sudden anti-sex movement on my part. It wasn't one of those situations where you end it with someone and you never have to see them again. We worked together. I had to see Nate every day and every day he hinted or told me how he wanted me six ways to Sunday…it was kind of fun to be wanted knowing I wasn't going to just give it up to him…trust me, it doesn't happen too often.

Nate wanted the relationship…I mean the sex…to continue and I kind of enjoyed saying no…for a while. One day, when everyone was out of the office, Nate tried getting frisky with me. I said no but he was frustrated, very frustrated. He was a walking hard-on. I kiddingly mentioned that I had lotion in my desk if he wanted to do it himself. He said great…he was desperate, but he said I had to watch. I agreed. I think Nate was hoping that I would join in or something, but at that point I don't think he cared how he got off, just as long as he did.

We went into Nate's office, sat on the couch, and he took his dick out. Within a few minutes, he started to complain about the smell…the lotion was floral scented. I wondered why he cared if his dick smelled like flowers, but I guess he likes his penis to smell manly. I, however, thought it was an improvement. The only problem with this set up is it started turning me on. At that point I wanted to attack, but since I was the one saying "no" I couldn't just change my mind and let Nate "win."

Nate was taking forever. I think he was just prolonging the inevitable orgasm hoping I would change my mind. I wasn't about to go back out on my "no" when I had worked so hard to get to that point. Nate didn't deserve me and I figured, if he wanted someone to join in, his girlfriend would suffice when he got home. Apparently she wasn't getting the job done in any department—let alone the sex department. Since he'd been cheating on her forever, I should have known that he wasn't getting the sexual attention that I knew he needed.

I thought of it this way: Nate giving himself a hand job in my presence was better than sending him packing with nothing to show for it except for blue balls and rejection to contend with. There was a little power in having a guy get so worked up that he has to just relieve his horniness in front of me…with me fully clothed and not participating in a sexual way. Well, except for watching, I guess that's voyeuristic. But if I was the one getting rejected, I wouldn't have dropped my pants and gone to town on myself. I would have salvaged a little dignity and left after throwing myself at some guy who was denying me my right to an orgasm.

Don't get me wrong I'm all for masturbation and self-satisfaction and there's nothing wrong with doing it in front of your partner. But after work, in the office, and after complete rejection? I'm not sure about that. Ah, I'm such a hypocrite…it was hot. It turned me on. I couldn't help it. I'd probably do it again too, but I think I'd end up giving in before the climax.

I actually know two adults who claim to have never masturbated. Luckily they just happen to be married to each other so they're the perfect couple. One of them told me that they think it's "disgusting and selfish"...whatever. I think life would be a lot different without that "disgusting" past time of masturbating. I don't know what I'd do without it and I think it's kind of weird not to. As Martha Stewart would probably say, "It's a good thing." She may not have meant that for self-satisfaction, but it's still a VERY good thing.

Eventually, I did start sleeping with my handy man again, but I made him wait until he'd dumped his girlfriend. I waited for an opportune time, his 40th birthday. Nate was determined to have sex with somebody and I couldn't let him do it with just anyone. I have some sympathy and compassion. After all, I did make him wait, which is so unlike me. It was either start sleeping with him again or spend all my free time pleasing myself...I wouldn't have accomplished anything that summer, so intercourse it was.

47

SPECIAL FINISH

Wouldn't you say that there's nothing better than a relaxing massage? Getting rubbed down, head to toe by someone who is a professional. One of my careers was a massage therapist, a masseuse. I worked in chiropractors' offices, at a day spa in Beverly Hills, and privately, where I would go to clients' homes to give them a massage. I did this for about five years as a professional, but have been doing it all my life as an amateur. I'm a natural at it, always have been. Either you got it or you don't in the massage world and I got it! When I was a little kid my older brother would pay me 50 cents to massage his back for half an hour. Even as a child, I didn't know my own worth. I obviously never learn.

I don't boast about too many things besides giving great BJs, but I will say I'm an amazing massage therapist. That's probably why I also can give an amazing hand job. Fortunately or unfortunately, depending on how you look at it, I quit the massage thing after I got bored. That and because I have this weird belief that massage therapy is just one step away from prostitution…actually it might be one step past. I would much rather have non-emotional sex with a complete stranger than touch their dirty naked bodies from head to toe AND do all of the work.

I know it's not a healthy belief, but it is my belief, so it kind of makes sense even if only to me. It doesn't help that I fit the stereotype of a massage prostitute, being Asian and all. I would have had a larger clientele if only I did perform the "special finish" or the "happy ending" like so many of my Asian massage parlor counterparts. I might as well go work for the Happy Finish Massage Palace. I'd probably fit in there much better. I'd most likely make more in tips there than anywhere else, especially since I do give such a good hand job.

Being propositioned, unfortunately, is part of the job…and it SUCKS. Lucky for me, I was only propositioned once by a client. Ben was a smelly euro-trash type and, from the minute he walked into the room, I had to hold my breath or breathe through my mouth to avoid getting sick. Thank God the massage didn't last long because Ben soon made it very obvious he didn't want JUST a massage…he kept moving my hands to inappropriate places. When his not-so-subtle hints didn't work, he asked for more. I said NO. He asked why I told him because it was against the law AND he couldn't pay me enough. I quickly realized that might not have been the most appropriate response because Ben then asked "How much?" At that point I ended the massage. Even though his scent lingered on, I was glad to be rid of him. I basically threw him off the table and asked that he not return. In hindsight, maybe I should have asked how much he was willing to pay. You never know, maybe it would have gotten me out of debt, or at least a lobster dinner. Kidding, the thought of that still makes me sick. YUCK.

Then there was the gentleman who started to hump the table the minute I started to massage his back. I'd never seen anyone do that before during a massage and I didn't know what to do at first. When I told him it wasn't "that kind of a massage," he said it relaxed him…he could have saved a lot of money and stayed at home if that's what "relaxed" him instead of getting a massage.

Being a massage therapist isn't ALL bad…there was another more pleasant incident, but Brad was a private client of mine. Cute, single, and older. We were becoming friends. At first we'd just hang out and talk after the massage, then he started ordering dinner for us. One night, unsurprisingly after the massage and dinner, he made a move on me. I wasn't sure if I'd have sex with him, I didn't want him thinking it was a part of "services rendered." The doubts went away pretty quickly. I fucked him of course…and it wasn't bad either. That also could have been because I hadn't had sex in six months. I was horny and desperate…desperate enough to not charge for the massage; I didn't want any blurry lines of prostitution and massage therapy. Even if I did charge, I'm sure I would have under-valued myself as usual.

A few days later Brad called for another massage, but instead of the usual massage he just got sex, which I was glad for because I couldn't charge him, but I definitely didn't want to give him another free massage. The client-massage therapist relationship didn't last long; we ended up getting in to an argument soon after the sex because Brad thought I was ripping him off by overcharging him for his massages…which I wasn't. Even if I was over-charging him for the massage, I figured it was a wash since I didn't charge him for the sex. Brad would never have been able to afford me if I did make him pay for both.

Since I "retired" from the biz as a masseuse, I have to admit it doesn't hurt in the dating realm. When I meet a good-looking guy with a hot body I quickly, but casually mention that I was a massage therapist. It's a great excuse to touch a guy all over, because they seem to inevitably welcome it, and because they always seem to have a sore back or neck or something else that needs a little attention. And I always oblige, except of course when they're boring and obnoxious, then I lay my trap for the next hot guy I meet. I don't give my massages away to just anybody…they have to earn it a little, or I have to at least want to fuck them!

On more than one occasion I've been lucky enough to have a hot naked man on my massage table for a little recreational massage. It's definitely a turn-on for me and a man never seems more grateful or horny than after a full body massage…especially if he knows a little sex and foreplay are to come. It's another power position that I enjoy and there's something to be said about having sex on a massage table. If you've never tried it, I highly recommend it. You can generally rent them at a massage supply store for about $20 a day. Take a suggestion from a seasoned professional, get a good tasting, lick-able massage oil—there's nothing worse than a bad tasting body after you've done all that work. You don't have to be a professional to act like one…men and women are very appreciative of the effort and it's great foreplay. TRUST ME!

48

I HAVE A HEADACHE

I love sex. Don't we all? It's a priority in my life, it always has been but at times a girl just doesn't feel like having sex…especially if it's with a partner you're just tired of or just plain hate. You can't exactly tell your partner that you're bored to death of them, can you? So creative excuses…or in my case, not-so-creative excuses have to be used. It might spare their feelings…even if just a little. Trust me, I'd rather be having good sex than saying NO…I guess that's why I rarely say "no." The optimist in me hopes for good sex every time.

In those boring relationships, I have been guilty of a few lame excuses. "I'm tired," sure. "I don't feel well," definitely. "I have to wake up early, honey," once in awhile, but the first time I heard "I have a headache" come out of my mouth to avoid sex I was shocked…it wasn't like me. I'm almost always up for sex. I couldn't believe I said such a stupid thing but at the time I was just in no mood to actually fuck my boyfriend. I was in college; we were at our sexual peeks and all I could think of was, "How am I going to get out of having sex with Carl this time?" It was the best I could come up with on such short notice…pathetic I know.

It's not like the sex was horrible or anything. It was actually kind of nice. I guess that's when our relationship started going downhill—when I lost interest in our sex life. Or I just realized two years was all the monogamy I could handle. I know how I feel when I get turned down, it fucking SUCKS. I can't imagine what it would feel like from a live-in girlfriend? Kind of like getting kicked in the ego, not to mention the heart. This kind of thing should be avoidable right? We should communicate better. We're adults, but I think that kind of honesty is just difficult for most women...or just for me? I don't know.

Maybe before crossing the sexual threshold there should be a conversation for setting up the rules of engagement. Like soccer, instead of penalty cards you could have sex excuse cards. The red card: "I don't want to have sex no matter what." Yellow card: "I'm not really in the mood, but if you do all the work I could get into it." Green card: "Don't ask and you won't get rejected." And, perhaps a black card: "Let's get down and dirty baby, anyway you like it!" You could just hang the cards above your side of the bed to let your partner know the status of your sex or non-sex mood. When there's no "card" it's just the normal, open for anything kind of mood. We could even expand the color card system to include, "I want to be tied up," "I want anal sex," "I want oral sex first," or "I want to use toys." For those who find telling their lover what they want to be difficult, this could be a great non-verbal way to get the message across.

When a man doesn't want to have sex with me they seem to be honest, too honest maybe...I always hear "I'm too tired" or "Maybe tomorrow" or "Not in your brother's house, I just met him." It's *always* something...I would just like a man with a little bit of a sex drive, even a normal one would be nice. Is that too much to ask? But, I suppose that if we women have to put up with the stupid reasons and excuses, shouldn't we at least get the honesty right too! No more lying. No more excuses. Just, "I don't want to have sex with you tonight" should suffice and if they want more you can tell them, "I don't feel like getting dirty right now" or "I need to take a shower and don't feel like it" or, "I'm just not in the mood honey, let's try it tomorrow."

I think it's fair to turn a partner down for sex once in awhile. Since we've all had sex when we don't feel like it, it should be a wash. No one's feelings should be hurt; it's just part of the game. You could keep score. "I had sex last week with you when I didn't feel like it, so you HAVE to have sex with me tonight, even if you're not in the mood." You'd be even. And that would be the end of the discussion. All's fair. I mean, especially if the orgasms are a lot more in favor of the man, which is very common…a woman should be able to say, "I'll only have sex with you if you give me at least one orgasm before you finish and go to sleep" and she should be able to pick the method and the position.

In addition, for every two of the man's orgasms women should be entitled to at least one…I'd be very happy with that equation. None of that 10 to 1 crap…that's why a lot of women don't want to have sex every time the man wants to because the man gets theirs no matter what. If we have something on our minds, or are stressed out, or you're not doing it right, some of us can't achieve our orgasms all the time, right girls? It's not fair, so we have to do our best to level the playing field. Quid pro quo…or we say NO!

In a good relationship, I am rarely not in the mood and even when I'm not in the mood, I'm usually more than willing to give a guy a mind blowing hummer or hand job to get him through if I don't actually want to have intercourse. I'll give a guy a blowjob even when he doesn't ask for one, like while he's watching footfall or something…because I'm in the mood. Although, maybe I should stop doing that…I've never had a guy go down on me while I'm watching a decorating or cooking show. It doesn't seem fair does it? I'm starting to think that the whole sex thing is unfair…especially since the older I get, the older the men I date get, which means the lower their sex drive gets, which means they want to have sex with me less and less. Maybe I should get headaches a little more often, torture them a little…nah, there's no fun in that either.

Since that first dreaded "headache" incident, I've really tried to be a little bit more truthful about my sexual desire. "I don't feel like it" generally works pretty well, with a promise of later or a blowjob or hand-job. That doesn't happen very often when you keep your relationship duration down to a nice minimum. Normally when they end, I still want more sex since that seems to be the basis and/or beginning of most of my "relationships." That and I have an insanely high sex drive and I use sex as a substitute for real, true intimacy. Just like a man! No need to say no when you always want sex, right?

PART VIII

49

JUST SEX, PLEASE!

Sex. No commitment. No emotion. Raw sex. Intercourse. Animal passion. Meeting a need. Just sex. Animalistic fucking. There's nothing wrong with having a sexual fling and not having it mean anything. Screw some guy's brains out and then send him packing. Or regularly fool around with the same guy, which is a favorite of mine, and have it mean nothing…its just sex.

My fuck buddy may not be like the traditional fuck-buddy relationship. I like to call what I do "Date Fucking." I do not, I repeat, DO NOT like to be called at 2 a.m. for sex, especially by a drunken fool looking to get laid just because I had sex with him on some other occasion. I like my sleep way too much to have it interrupted. If I wanted to get laid that night I would have planned for it better than waking up to a ringing phone. If you want to have sex with me it's going to cost you at least a couple of drinks and/or a little conversation. I guess it's just because I like to be warmed up a little bit before I jump into JUST SEX. If it's someone I'm involved with, I don't need more than a "hello" for an appetizer.

I actually asked a guy I was hanging out with once if he wanted to "date me or fuck me, because either way I wasn't in the mood." I wanted to know because we were hanging out, spending time together as "friends," etc. etc. Nothing had happened yet, but I knew eventually something would and I wanted to be clear on what was or wasn't about to happen. Drew just said he wanted to have a little fun…whatever that could lead to…meaning he didn't want a relationship to begin with, just sex. I was happy to know we were on the same page.

I've probably had too many fuck-buddies, but it satisfies my need for sex without the commitment. I don't like going too long without it, so I rotate the regulars and repeats, which are all fuck-buddies of course, but most of them are my friends too. I'd rather do it with the same guy every once in a while than do it with random guys and have it suck, or worse yet catch something in the process. My list would just be too long if I did that and I like it the way it is.

I used to have a fuck-buddy who is still on my Top 10 list of best in bed. He was great. Carter was always very passionate and a very good kisser. He'd call me. We'd meet for drinks at some out of the way bar. We'd get drunk. We'd race back to my place and, before we got through the door, Carter would be all over me. More than once, we almost got it on in my hallway. We'd have mad sex for hours…always more than once and often the next morning. He'd always see my furniture in a new way…Carter would find more uses for a normal chair than any guy I knew. He was absolutely great…I kind of miss it to be honest, but it was too good to be true.

You'd think my being easy and all, I would be completely okay with JUST SEX. I am, most of the time. Sometimes, I'm not. It all depends on the man and the situation. I cannot spend time with a man, have him take me out to dinner and spend time on the phone talking to him, then go home have some fantastic sex and never get attached. That's insane. It's impossible for me and I think that's too much to ask of any woman. Men are better at separating but, come on, don't guys have feelings too? I mean, give a girl a break. If you just want to have sex with her, booty-call her. Don't "date" her. Just fuck her, please! It's not fair and it's not playing by the rules. If you don't want anything except for sex, tell her. If you want to be just her friend, don't fuck her. My date fucking is different, the whole point of the "date" is to fuck…everyone know's what they are getting. Everyone wins!!

I feel I must educate, because I've learned recently that some people out there don't understand the fuck buddy rules. So, just in case you want to avoid a potentially hurtful situation or you're looking to add a fuck-buddy to your arsenal or you just need to be reminded of the do's and don'ts, I'll surmise what I believe to be the basic rules of "fuck-buddydom."

- *No kissing*—outside of the fucking or pre-hook-up.

- *No dates*—except to meet for sex, maybe drinks to make the morals a little looser and the guilt less but absolutely no dinner…just sex.

- **No talking outside of encounters except to set up the next encounter**—no long conversations about your childhood, or what you did today unless it leads to why you want sex or anything else with sexual content.

- *No expectations*—don't expect to date them, don't expect them to change their mind, **and don't fall in love with them**. It'll never work out.

- *No two nights in a row*—that's self-explanatory

- *No staying the night* (This is a flexible rule.)—But if they stay, NO CUDDLING! NO CUDDLING! NO CUDDLING! And there MUST be morning sex for a sleep over…that is not negotiable.

- *No giving them a toothbrush*—they can leave with morning breath for all you care.

- *No making breakfast for them*—the next morning, or ever, for that matter. No domestication allowed.

Those are the hard and fast rules. Simple, but pretty straight forward. I never thought I'd have to explain the rules to a man, but there's a first for everything. The less confusing the better. If you need more fuck-buddy rules, there are great "Booty Call Agreements" on the Internet. I highly suggest getting them, reading them, memorizing them, and learning to live by them for the rest of your booty-calling, fuck-buddy lives.

No one should go to their grave without having at least one fuck-buddy in their life. It's unnatural not to have one when you're in-between relationships or sexually in a lull. But if you're going to participate as a fuck-buddy, know what you are. Know what your "relationship" really is. Don't think it's going anywhere, because, odds are, it won't. Not that I'm not guilty of turning a fuck-buddy into a short-term relationship, but I try not too. Generally, the fuck-buddy relationship lasts longer than my normal relationships. I've had the same fuck-buddy off and on for over three years. In the beginning I liked him because there was this deep physical attraction. It didn't take me long before I knew that there wasn't anything more to it than sex, lots of great sex…well that and lots of alcohol too, which always helps.

50

DON'T KID YOURSELF

I need to practice what I preach, I really should. I admit it; I'm guilty of growing fond of men who only want me for sex. I'm guilty of expecting men, who are getting sex by just calling me up and coming over, to want me for more than just sex. I'm guilty for hoping that these men will eventually like me. I'm guilty of kidding myself that relationships based purely on sex will become more. As I've gotten older, one thing on my side is that I'm *slowly* learning from my mistakes…or the very least, I'm recognizing that I have this reoccurring bad behavior that just won't go away.

Andrew, a long time acquaintance, asked me on a real date once before we were fuck buddies. We talked all night, got hammered, went back to my place, and fooled around…meaning I gave him a blowjob and he ate me out. I didn't hear from him and, for a silly moment, I actually thought it was because we had oral sex, that he would think I was easy, or not the kind of girl to have a relationship with. Funny thing is, I would have had sex with him, but I think our friendship weird-ed him out a little. It knocked the silly right out of me and I realized I wasn't a teenager anymore, and putting out a little rarely makes a difference…and if it did, I wouldn't want to date that kind of hypocritical guy in the first place.

When I finally did speak to Andrew he said that he decided it would ruin our baseless friendship if we dated or fooled around or whatever but in reality he wanted his ex back. A couple of weeks later I went to an early dinner with some friends and he was there; the chemistry was definitely still there. We flirted like mad. There had always been sexual tension between us, but that night it was like electricity. It didn't help that I got a taste of what could come from a sexual encounter with him. For me, it added to the attraction and I knew something tawdry was in my future...there always is.

During dinner we all discussed meeting for drinks later...not everyone was interested in going but Andrew and I were. We made a date to meet later, not sure if anyone else would show, but we didn't care. I went home and after a power-nap and a fresh pre-sex bathing I was off to meet him. No one else showed up...it was just Andrew and I. I was excited. I knew he wanted me as much as I wanted him, I just didn't know what was going on with his high school love, but I guess he was looking for a little sexual action in the meantime.

We had a good time and got liquored up—just enough to let our guard down and allow our horns to come out. The bar was closing and we walked outside together. We attempted to say our awkward good-byes but instead we just stood there, waiting for someone to make the first move...and since I rarely make that move, I waited...Andrew asked me if I wanted to go hang out some more... I said "Sure," but at the time I didn't realize that "Do you wanna go hang out?" actually meant, "Do you want to have sex?" Which we did, A LOT. I just wish he had been a little more clear and upfront, not that I still wouldn't have said YES, because I definitely would have. But at least I would have known what to expect...some of the most fantastic sex I've ever had! Thank God for "hanging out!"

From then on out we would have a sexual encounter at least weekly. It was a really nice way to pass the time and we'd have a lot of fun when we went out too, which I guess was part of the problem for me. Not that Andrew was boyfriend material, he was selfish, egotistical, he smoked way too much, including pot, he was too hung up on a lost love, etc. But he didn't want me, so that made him the perfect guy for me at the time.

He would call me up after I hadn't heard from him for a month or two. It got to the point where I didn't believe that he was calling just to say "hi" or to catch up, but he was calling for sex. I would cut through the crap and just ask him, "Andrew, are you horny? Is that why you're calling?" He'd get defensive and reply, "What, I can't call my 'friend' once in awhile?" I'd let him get away with this defense. We'd make plans to go for drinks, and then we'd end up having sex. It would always turn out that he just broke up with someone and needed his regular sex buddy back...HIM, predictable. ME, gullible.

The next time Andrew called, I allowed the friend thing and didn't have sex with him. We'd hang out once or twice a week. It worked for about a month until we slept together...surprise surprise. Then it was kind of pointless pretending we were just friends and not fuck-buddies. Everything we did had an underlying sexual tension to it. We couldn't have coffee without it just hanging there above our heads...instead of having amazing mind blowing sex; we'd be sitting there having a drink, just TALKING. How boring! He was more fun to fuck. Unfortunately, if you confuse the fuck-buddy situation by making it murky then someone's going to get hurt. I'm a chick. If the sex is good, and the sex was GOOD, the guy is nice, and you like hanging out with each other then what else is there to be desired in a relationship?

However, you really have to watch what you wish for because you may actually get your wish and regret every minute of it. My favorite fuck buddy decided he wanted more than just sex from me, he wanted to DATE ME! Which wasn't a big leap, I guess. Every time we hung out it felt like a date but without the commitment. At first I was a little excited about the evolution of our "relationship." That excitement was short-lived. The minute he got emotionally attached to me, the sex got bad...really bad. Instead of fucking on the living room floor he went to the scary place of, "Would you like to go to the bedroom?" for boring missionary position sex. Since when does relationship have to mean boring? Wait a minute! I think that's Webster's Dictionary's definition for relationship...BORING SEX. Unfortunately this was partially my fault, I had at this point thought that dating him would be great, great sex, great fun, great friendship all rolled into one...but I was wrong...very wrong.

The good thing is I always know that when I'm between sex partners, I can always count on someone. Maybe I should call one now...I'm a little horny and could use a good shagging! Especially by someone who knows all of my erotic buttons.

51

MORNING SEX

Some people think the best way to start the morning is with a big hot steaming cup of coffee. I, however, prefer a big hot smoking man and raunchy sex. And since I don't drink coffee, a good hard man is sometimes the only thing that can get me out of bed in the morning. Unfortunately for me there isn't an available man at every corner like there is a Starbucks or Coffee Bean. If only I could franchise morning sex like the coffee industry…I'd be a millionaire and I'd be getting all of the sex I want too. Life couldn't be more perfect.

Recently I had some amazing morning sex with Robert, a fuck-buddy. I had no intention of having sex with him, even though we had three bottles of wine and crawled into bed together. I thought we'd just sleep, which is basically all we did. The only reason he didn't put any moves on me the night before was because we both passed out from being drunk and tired. There's something to be said for being awakened by a hard cock and groping hands. Even then, I actually thought I would say "no," just to be hard to get once in awhile, but I couldn't resist. He's just got too big of a cock.

The only problem with morning sex is morning breath…you either avoid each other's mouths like they're black holes, missing out on an enjoyable part of sex, or you grin and bare it, dealing with the lethal fumes emanating from your partner's mouth. It really is a bummer. I've begun keeping those Listerine strips next to the bed—just in case a big hard dick awakens me for a nice morning shag. A girl has to be prepared.

This time, we dealt with the morning breath and made out like crazy. Robert's a great kisser and, since I didn't get any action the night before, I wanted the entire package. Head to toe attention…six and nine, front and back, etc. I couldn't have asked for anything more. Robert's never been a wham-bam kind of guy; I almost always get the entire body treatment from him. If I didn't, I would never have kept him around as long as I did.

It had been almost a year since the last time I slept with him, not that he hadn't tried a few times, but I wasn't really in the mood. The last time Robert tried putting the moves on me he was pretty blunt—asked me if I'd put him "in my schedule." I think that's the nicest way anyone has ever asked me to be their fuck-buddy. Don't beat around the bush, just say it, "I want to fuck you often with absolutely no strings attached." How easy!

I would keep fucking Robert forever if he could guarantee me mind-blowing sex every morning…it would be worth all of the potential heartaches and headaches. Not to mention making my life a lot easier and work much more enjoyable if I started every day with a male-given orgasm. Like I said earlier, if only I could bottle it…a night of body heat, cuddling and morning sex…I'd be a rich, *satisfied* woman.

52

BI ON THE SIDE

I love gay men. Some of my best friends are gay. They tell you that you look fabulous. They compliment your shoes. They notice your clothes. They set you up with the straight guys they know that they can't have…what could be better? That said, closeted men should stay away from women with bad taste. At least until they decide what they want: women or men. I realize it can be hard to come out, but if you have any suspicion that you might like men more than me, please stay away. I really don't need the headache. I have a bad enough time with men without being hit on by men who might like a penis more than a vagina.

Along with my lack of "gaydar," the ability to sort the straight guys from the gay or bi ones, it enables me to be in bad situation after bad situation. I feel like men, whether straight or gay, either ignore me or they go completely out of their way to meet me—especially the really freaky ones. I know I'm not the only one who feels like this, but it's always in the last place you expect a man to make a little effort when they do. I always expect a come-on in the supermarket, at a bar, in a club, at the mall, you know, normal places. But I get the ones who climb over restaurant booths to get my attention, or hit on me while I'm on a date, or at work by my bosses. I would just like a normal situation where a man can feel comfortable approaching me, is that too much to ask?

Walking from my car to work one morning, I saw a cute guy in a convertible. He saw me too. Actually he was staring at me. I smiled and when the light changed, I went on my way, forgetting the flirtation. A couple minutes later I was about to walk into the spa where I worked when he was honking his horn and flipping a U-turn in the middle of a very busy street trying to get my attention. He jumped out of his car, introduced himself as Tim, and asked me if I'd go to coffee with him. He was cute. I was flattered. He was late for work and I would be too if we went for coffee, so we made plans for lunch later that day.

We had a great time at lunch and talked for hours, he took me to my car and barely kissed me goodbye. I wanted more. We made plans to go out the next night too. We went to a bar on Sunset Boulevard and had quite a few drinks. We kissed in the bar some, then ran across the busy street and crashed a fancy restaurant's reservation list. Tim was a manager at a five-star hotel and pulled "rank" on the host. It was so cool at the time considering how drunk I was and how infatuated I had become. Unfortunately, throughout our involvement that is the only thing that impressed me.

Drunk and horny, we went back to my place. By the time we got to the bedroom, we were both naked and ready for action. It was pretty hot and heavy for about two weeks, but from there our "relationship" went downhill. I should have known that his obsession with penises—and not just his own—was a sign. My *gaydar* has always been a little off, but I was starting to get a weird vibe from him. I actually asked him if he was gay a couple of times, he just said that's what his ex-wife used to say. I wonder why?

We went out for about four months before I finally ended it, very immaturely, over the phone, because, he was spending most of his time at Rage, a gay club in West Hollywood, with his roommate who had just come out of the closet. I'm sure if I had a penis, Tim would have paid just as much attention to me as he did his gay counterparts.

We started up again about six months later. It was mostly sexual at that point, mostly anal sex. He confessed to me that when we first started dating he was still married…supposedly the divorce papers hadn't gone through. Now divorced, he could love freely…just not me. This perverted sexual relationship went on unsteadily for about a year and a half longer. At times we would lose touch, but then he'd show up at my apartment uninvited and unannounced. I was working nights and he was working long days so I thought it was natural we didn't see each other that often.

Toward the end of our association, Tim was being transferred to a San Diego hotel and was having a good-bye party…the same weekend as the gay pride parade. He invited me over. We had sex while everyone was outside, then he went out and hit on one of his old co-workers. I confronted him and told him it was bullshit and he reassured me by making out with me. The party was mostly made up of bi-sexual males and gay guys pretending to be straight…I was being hit on by most of the closeted males at the party.

On the spur of the moment, everyone migrated to another party in Hollywood. I left my car and purse behind because Tim said we'd only be gone for a little bit. I would soon regret that decision. The new party location was on the roof of an apartment building, where Tim snuggled up to another "straight" guy while I froze. I asked one of the tenants to take me to get a sweatshirt and when I came back Tim was gone. Everyone I had known at the party was gone. It was hours until I conned someone from the party to take me back to my car.

I arrived back at Tim's to retrieve my purse and car at about three in the morning. Good thing for him he wasn't there, because I really think I would have ripped his eyes out if I got a hold of him. I was lucky, kind of, his gay roommate was there and subtly outted him to me…at least I knew I wasn't imagining things. Only I could date or sleep with someone and be so blinded by bad taste and not know he was bisexual. I'm at times still in shock at how gullible I was and still am. How thoroughly stupid I was, really! No really!

The incident with Tim wasn't the only gay-guy-in-hiding I've encountered. Terry was another. Oddly enough Tim and Terry overlapped. I was sleeping with both of them around the same time. Apparently I love the abuse. The last one thought it was perfectly okay to take a shower with seven naked men and one woman at his house. There were rumors that he was gay all along, but as usual, I chose to ignore the signs. Or more likely, I recognized the signs of bad taste and went full steam ahead.

As if his confessions of naked man showering weren't bad enough, his being my boss and telling everyone in the office about our so-called sex life sealed my title of "worst taste in the world". Adding insult to injury, he had a hairy back and a small penis, but according to him a beautiful penis, drove a Porsche to over-compensate, and very very bad taste in clothes. Put me out of my misery and shoot me now, please.

Like it's not bad enough, there was Harding who once told me I gave him the best blowjob he'd ever had from a GIRL! I later got a full confession that he knew firsthand that men give better blowjobs than women. Apparently that's not all he got from guys. Harding said he didn't consider himself gay or bi-sexual, rather a "tri-sexual," he'd *try* anything once…but he was trying guys a lot more than just once. He wasn't into guys romantically, like kissing and cuddling, just the sexual stuff…supposedly. I guess I'm just too insecure for that kind of thing, you can't compete really if you don't have what it takes anatomically. Even though, I'm ready and willing to strap one on for a guy, sometimes that's just not good enough for them…it's not like I'm not a team player. I'm just not really willing to watch them get it in the ass from another guy. I'm very willing to please my man, but only within reason!

Since these incidences, I have come up with a not so fool-proof test for bi-sexuality: When you're in a group of people who can be honest with each other and/or comfortable, casually ask, "Have you or would you ever get a blowjob from a guy?" Normally, the group will respond in a negative way. But at times the person you are secretly testing will either be the most silent person in the group, or he will be overly protesting that under absolutely no circumstance would he never, ever, ever allow such a thing to happen.

I have put this test to the test…I asked a man I knew had gotten a BJ from a guy once when he was high on coke. He didn't know I knew and I asked the question…he was the only one in the group who didn't say a word. He just sat back looking guilty. Maybe this guy wasn't a full bi-sexual, but I have to avoid any possibility of a guy switching teams on me. My average is just too high to take the risk especially since an ex of mine came clean about his bi-sexuality after we started dating…I was devastated. At least now I've got a way to weed out some of the guys on the fence…it's not fool proof, but it's better than nothing.

I mean it's okay if you're not ready to come out of the closet. You should do it when you're ready to face the world, but don't make me the target of your attempt to prove your heterosexuality. I could definitely do without the headache and I'm sure other girls would say the same. Especially since

I know I'm not the only girl in this predicament...I have more friends that I can count that have had similar incidence happen to them. I, personally, would rather know that you're confused in advance so I at least know what I'm getting into...but I guess it's not too realistic to ask for advance notice that you're in the closet. Oh, what's a girl to do?

53

FETISH FREAKS

I can't imagine getting pleasure from having a man peeing on me or having the desire to be spanked on the ass with celery. I'm not saying that I don't enjoy a little kinky sex once in awhile. Who doesn't enjoy being tied up or spanked once in awhile? To date, I do not have any certified fetishes, just an odd desire once in awhile…well maybe having my feet rubbed and toes sucked on, but who doesn't like that occasionally? I don't do anything often enough or want anything bad enough to qualify as a fetish. I think my only fetish is sleeping with complete losers and commitment-phobic men. If there isn't such a fetish, there should be. I could be the first test case.

I had a boyfriend who exercised his fetish on me by wrapping me in Saran Wrap when I was naked. When Clark did it, I was in complete shock. We were in his living room and he asked that I get naked. I obliged. At that point, he blindfolded me with a makeshift blindfold, which I think was a sock or something. I was getting excited. I had no idea what Clark was going to do, I was definitely intrigued but being wrapped in plastic was the last thing on my mind. I was hoping for something a little bit more stimulating.

Clark began to wrap me up, after fondling me for a while. He had me stand up while he wrapped me. I didn't know exactly what he was doing, but I trusted him and allowed him to finish. It took forever. While he was getting turned on, I was getting bored. Clark took my blindfold off for the "unveiling." I wasn't sure if I was supposed to be excited or not, so I just kind of stood there like an idiot waiting for him to do something. He just looked at me...in awe.

After a few minutes of him looking at me and telling me how hot I looked, he said it was time to cut me out of it. He laid me on the coffee table, left the room, and returned with a very large knife. I should have been scared...now that I think about it, I was. Clark began cutting the Saran Wrap off me slowly...too slowly. Besides it being very annoying, I could feel the blade against my skin and wanted it to be over quick. I wouldn't let a guy I just met do that to me or get anywhere near me with a knife, but this was my boyfriend so I let him.

After I was freed from my silly little outfit, Clark wanted to have sex where I lay...on the coffee table. At least until the front door opened and his roommate walked in. He reacted like he'd seen this before, which I'm sure he had, and just passed us by without even a nod. I think it was a fitting end to an interesting but stressful escapade. I could go the rest of my life without ever being dressed in plastic wrap again...I'm just thankful it didn't get any weirder. Clark never even tried to do it again, but I was glad that I could satisfy his kinky need to wrap me up like that once. As long as it isn't disgusting or painful, I'll let the guy I'm involved with act out his fantasies with me, but now I make them tell me about it first, so I know what I'm getting into.

The funny thing is that a few weeks later I was listening to the radio and the hosts were talking about a girl they knew who liked being wrapped in Saran Wrap...so much that she liked to almost be mummified in it—not able to move her arms or legs. She would just have her boyfriend cut a hole in the appropriate spot so he could stick his dick in. Now that's fucking funny, but I would definitely draw the line there...I wish it would have turned me on that way, but it didn't.

I mean, how do you figure out that you like something like that? Or, one of those other fetishes, like plushophilia (love for or sex with plushies, as in stuffed animals)? I can't imagine how you develop a liking for something like that, but I guess they could say the same thing about some of the things I like. There is so much weird crap out there that I can't begin to understand why some things turn on some and not others, but I'm into experimentation so maybe I will figure it out someday…or at least discover a fetish or two of my own.

I do know a guy who wants to use a sex swing with me, but that sounds really fun and I would definitely be up for that. Ken also wants to go toy shopping, which I haven't done in a long time, so I would be up for that too. I like guys who take that kind of control of the sexual activities I'm involved in. It makes it fun and exciting. If a man doesn't know how to experiment then how can the sex stay fresh and appealing? But if I am ever to settle down with a man "permanently," then I have to know that the sex will be good and have the potential for getting even better. So, sex swing here I come, or any other adventure Ken's up for. Be open, be free to experiment…you never know, you might discover you like it.

54

SUPER STAR SEX

*I*f you had the chance to hook up with a major, sexy, single, action star you would do it wouldn't you? He's rich, he's attractive, he's famous…You'd DIE HARD for him…I did! What's stopping you? Who in their right mind wouldn't fuck a guy like that? Well, apparently, I wouldn't. I would avoid the typical Hollywood behavior; I would not be a Star Fucker. I would not have sex with a star just to have sex with a star, no matter how big the star was or how bad I wanted to, even if I had a SIXTH SENSE about him. It could have been my first real one-night stand, but I was too stupid to do it. I just turned my nose up at him and looked the other way.

I think that I'm just afraid that someone who could have anyone wouldn't really want me, even if it were just to fuck. It's silly because I'm sure a lot of guys who have women throwing themselves at them all day, just fuck all the time, no matter the girl. Not really being picky, never really saying "no," right? I guess I have always wanted to be a little different, set myself apart a little by saying "no." Funny I can't say no to an average guy, but give me a super star and that's the first thing I do. The irony…it sucks.

It doesn't help when said star has you summoned by his bodyguard. I get turned off easily and was apt to say "NO" when the HELP is asking ME for the "date." If someone who is famous, rich, and successful can't make the little effort himself on his own behalf to court a woman, even if it is just to have sex, then what man is capable of it? I sure as hell wasn't going to throw myself at him, like every other girl in the bar. I reserve the honor of making an ass out of myself and throwing myself at the true losers in the world. My bad taste is always working against me…when I acknowledge a hot great guy is in my presence, I avoid him like the plague.

I said "no" to someone who I could have fantasized about for the rest of my life. You never know, it could have led to something beyond mind blowing sex if I would have just given him a chance, but I was trying to be different from the rest of the easy women…and there are a lot of us. My friends were shocked by my behavior. They fully expect me to sleep with a guy like that, and be able to recount every moment for them, allowing them to live vicariously through me. You see what happens when I try to say "no," when I go against my easy nature, I lose a fantastic opportunity. Even if for only one night. It's a story I could have disclosed many times with the envy of many others, but I'll probably never have that opportunity again. A lot of my friends thought I was stupid, for not just being the slut I want to be and sleeping with him. The minute I left the bar, I regretted it. I wanted him. I wanted him bad. He's one of the sexiest men in movies and I lost my opportunity… my motto is: when opportunity knocks, SPREAD YOUR LEGS!

My so-called Star Fucker days didn't begin there. I had the misfortune of, and the bad judgment of saying "No" to an action hero, and "Yes" to a kids show "action star" or "action actor," if acting is what you'd call what he did and he wasn't really a "star." I do have to admit he was beautiful to look at—kind of Rob Lowe meets Barney. I wish he would have had more Barney because I assume Barney would have been better in bed, or least had a big purple dick, because oh my God was this guy bad.

When I met Tad, I thought he was kidding when he said he worked on "the show." I actually made fun of him…a lot, until I realized he wasn't kidding. He said it was just a job to pay the bills until his real acting career kicked in. I did hear about him once when I found out he had slept with an acquaintance of mine. I reported to her that Tad was no Power Ranger in bed and she reported the same lackluster performance when she was with him, too. She, however, didn't make the mistake of having awful sex with him a second time; I did.

The funny thing is that he autographed a picture of himself in uniform for my little brother, who at the time, was a fan of the show. It still hangs on his wall, a constant reminder of my "star fucker" days. I think I'm done with the action genre for now, and look for my next opportunity to say "no" to someone really hot, rich, and famous, but if I could do it all over again, I wouldn't have sex with the B-TV star and I would with the super star...I like older men anyhow, and I'm sure it would have been much better. Lesson learned.

55

TOYS FOR GOOD GIRLS

I believe that every single girl needs a bag of toys to tide her over between encounters or to spice things up. It doesn't really matter, as long as you have a way to release. Good porn never hurts either. I deserve a good Christmas. I hope Santa knows that I can be naughty but very nice and I want some presents that will help me be even naughtier. I think it's very healthy to get a little extra helping hand when you're in need of a little manual release or when your lover needs that extra boost. They're fun. They're exciting. And they never get tired.

Below is a list of must-have toys for EVERY girl:

1. **Vibrators**—Assorted shapes and sizes—including the "Rabbit" (my favorite), it NEVER lets me down, EVER!

    Always, always have extra batteries on hand…the last thing you want to do is run out at a climatic moment!

2. **Dildos**—Sometimes a girl just wants a big old cock and when a real one can't be had. This is the next best thing! And they come in ALL sizes and colors!

3. **Butt plugs**—You have to have an assortment of shapes and sizes. Sometimes I'm in the mood for a *little* something…and other times, a BIG something!

4. **Vibrating butt plugs**—Hustler makes a fabulous one that vibrates and pulses at variable speeds, with the remote control close to your finger tips!

5. **Vibrating & heated nipple clamps**—One of my favorite birthday presents…when a man doesn't give the "girls" the attention they deserve, do it yourself!

6. **Cock rings**—Might want to have a various sizes on hand…Just in case the man in your life needs a little lift!

7. **Handcuffs**—Mine are of the furry variety, all of the comfort and none of the pain…with all of the bondage pleasure.

8. **Various other Bondage Equipment**—Old ties, belts, scarves, or anything else you can think of will work as great tie downs! Whatever gives you that feeling of restraint so you can lose control.

9. **Furry Blindfold**—Comfortable and not hard on the eyes…not to mention, there is no peeking in these! But when these can't be used, a bandana will suffice.

10. **Flavored and non-flavored lubricants**—Everybody needs a little extra glide once in a while, not to mention it's great for anal sex, anytime!

    *(Flavored, for a little lick-able fun; non-flavored, for the times you don't **want** to lick.)*

11. **Vibrating wire-free remote control panties**—I don't have these yet, but I'm hoping I'll get them someday soon. They sound FUN!

You can never have too many toys, I'm up for trying almost any of them.

It's not always easy for a "good girl" to get the nerve up to buy a toy. Thank God for the Internet! Back when I was in college, I would be sent to the local sex shop with a "shopping list" from my friends who were too embarrassed, or afraid, to even enter the store. I never cared really…it was fun to people-watch and to check out the great gadgets. I did experience a hint of embarrassment on one of my shopping excursions when I was sent to buy four vibrators. I entered the store, checked out the equipment, and picked just the right sizes and colors. I went to the register, laid down the four vibrators and threw in a pair of furry handcuffs for myself. I started to think that this guy must think I go through these things faster than anyone he'd ever seen…either that or he was thinking that I didn't really have four places to put them at the same time, unless I was into lesbian orgies or something.

The embarrassment was silly. The cashier looked at me like any other customer. I'm sure he'd seen it all. It's like going to the gynecologist…you're not that much different than the last vagina that came through the door, and the same goes for sex stores. If you've never ventured into a pleasure store, your first step should be to just go in—just to look, or wait until you have a valid excuse…bachelor/bachelorette party…that way you don't feel like a pervert looking to buy yourself some toys. Most sex shops have a fantastic array of novelty and gag gifts too, so if you feel you have to buy something on your first visit, but can't make the luxury purchase, buy a chocolate penis or some edible undies.

When you do go in, you'll realize everyone there is basically normal. But find a store that isn't too seedy on your first run…even though the seedy ones have better prices and a funkier selection. I find that it's liberating to buy your first sex toy. Go to the counter look them in the eye and say, "Wrap up that dildo for me, please, and toss in a tube of anal lube while you're at it." Trust me, I have friends my age that I still have to go to the store and buy condoms for. You don't want to be thirty and still not be able to buy a jumbo pack of Trojans when the need arises…I go to Costco or Sam's Club and stock up on them so I don't have to buy every other day.

I produced a radio show that gave away a sexual novelty item called Gummydongs as one of our prizes (www.gummydongs.com). Gummydongs are edible vibrators. They're not completely edible; they have a sugar-free gummy bear type coating over a small, powerful vibrator. All of my friends wanted one so I made them call into the show to "win" one by doing all sorts of wacky things. There shouldn't be anything embarrassing about wanting a sex toy, but thankfully, back then, I could make it embarrassing for them to win. There's got to be some fun in giving away sex toys, besides the fun of knowing my friends and peers are out gettin' their own.

If you haven't noticed yet, I'm kind of a control freak. I've finally come to terms with this ailment of mine, but I've found that even though I like being in control in my everyday life, I do not like to be in control in the bedroom. Why would I? I have to make sure everything else in my life is in order. Why wouldn't I want to just sit back and relax when the lights go out…Well, I like the lights on most of the time, but you get the idea. I like the man to take over, tell me what to do, be in complete control of the situation…and that includes handcuffing me up once in awhile, and blindfolding me if necessary.

When I get handcuffed, while totally naked, it can be such a rush, wrists bound above the head, ankles strapped down, all I can do is just take whatever my man wants to do to me. Actually I love it. I recently purchased some bondage "equipment" and it's done wonders, especially since I do not have a headboard, so it's a little more difficult to be tied, other than the traditional handcuff method. They're "Rachel's Cumfy Cuffs" and they can be used on any bed or anything you want to strap yourself down to. I love these things. I keep them near my bed at all times, just in case a spur of the moment bondage session pops up. Unfortunately for me, it doesn't pop up often enough…when I bought them, I had a boyfriend who claimed he liked that kind of thing. Not once did he ever use them; I was extremely disappointed. Here's a hint, if your partner buys bondage gear or suggests it, it means they really want you to tie them up…don't make them beg. Well, don't make them beg unless it's a turn on.

Just like so many other things in my life I do not want any hand-me-downs, which means I don't want to "use" anything USED…unless it's used by me. I don't know if men have problems with hand-me-downs or previously used "couples" items, but I can't tolerate any used toys in my bedroom. It would be like going to the Good Will of sex toys and picking up a not-so-sanitized vibrator, not knowing who the last owner was and how exactly it was previously used. I guess men really don't have this problem very often since 99% of the toys are used on *us*…I'll bet if *they* were forced to use a second-hand cock ring or butt plug *they* might feel differently. Maybe in my next "relationship" I should experiment with this notion…I'll pull out a sex toy and tell them I used it on a guy or two before them and test whether they have an issue with it.

The first time a guy whipped a toy out on me I was blindfolded and all I could hear is the buzz of what I assumed was a vibrator—which I was thankfully right about—but in the throws of passion all I could think to do was start an uncomfortable conversation that went something like this:

Me: Um…is that new?

Gene: Of course.

Me: (skeptical) Okay, I just want to make sure you've never used it on *anyone* else.

Gene: I just bought it for you…I swear! Do you want to see the receipt?

Me: (finally able to relax) No, you may continue.

He continued and I was able to enjoy myself. He must have known about this "phenomenon," because when we broke-up he offered the toy up to me. Like a moron, I didn't take it like I should have, because I thought having one at home was enough…I didn't realize at the time that it would have been nice to own a couple options. Hopefully he didn't get more use out of it by trying it on the next unsuspecting girl. But really, what is a guy supposed to do with used sex toys if the girl doesn't take them with her? There should be some sort of recycling program for men with used sex toys… maybe they could get a tax credit for every turned in toy, used or unused. That would be fair. I would vote for this tax break so it could potentially spare me from being the victim of a tainted vibrator.

I generally don't whip things out of my own "hardware" collection with guys. It can be very intimidating for some men. Actually I've only done it once and we didn't use it. Apparently Jack wasn't impressed with my selection. We did go toy shopping very soon after and got some fun equipment. Toys and accessories are the best. I would love to have my own line of sexual aids. It would be great—an unlimited supply of NEW toys. I could test every prototype and give it either a "Screaming—O" recommendation for leg-shaking pleasure, or just a slight "Moaning O," sufficient when alone, but not a man replacement. I'm sure I've got one or two new inventions up my skirt for the sexually adventurous kind…or maybe for the not so adventurous that are dying to be a little more daring. Any investors interested in my Yummi-Teaz Line just let me know…I'll be the spokes model and tester.

56

FORBIDDEN FRUIT

Brothers…not my brothers…two men who are brothers. The forbidden fruit? The unthinkable? During college I dated, I mean slept with, brothers, two very hot brothers. Not at the same time, but I had sex with them within weeks of each other. I'm not quite that easy—to have a threesome with two brothers—it might be just a little too creepy for even me—or at least it was at the time.

I'd been sleeping with the younger one, Carey, for a couple years. I think I was infatuated with him from the minute we met; he was beautiful…exactly what I would want my imaginary husband to look like. The sex was always hot and kind of forbidden in and of itself. He was friends with my ex-boyfriend, who wasn't quite over me yet. Carey and I would meet in dive bars and other out-of-the-way places at school so no one we knew would see us together. The secret rendezvous always made it much more exciting…I always looked forward to our meetings. I'm sure if everyone knew about us, I wouldn't have been as interested.

I couldn't get enough of him sexually, but I wanted more from him than I could get…as always. He was still hung up on his ex-girlfriend and didn't want more than sex and friendship from me. No matter what I did he never wanted more, so I gave him all the sex he wanted, that was some-thing at least...especially since it was GOOD sex. Dragging it out for years, every once in awhile I would get my hopes up just to have them destroyed.

That's about the time I met Jason, Carey's older brother...I thought Carey was beautiful, but Jason was amazing. We hung out for a while as friends, and we had fun together, getting to know each other. At the time, Carey and I were kind of on hiatus...which would happen from time to time. We wouldn't see each other for a while, and then we'd hook up again, when we were between "relationships" or if we were bored. Jason and I were just friends, mostly because he didn't know about Carey and me. I always felt that if I slept with Jason it would ruin it for Carey and me forever—that is, if he found out. Not that there was any hope of anything real ever hap-pening between Carey and me...but I still hoped.

I liked Jason a lot. He was kind. He was fun. And he didn't just want to fuck me, he wanted to get to know me. We had a lot of fun just hanging out together. I did want to have sex with him, I really did, but at that time the most we ever did was kiss once. The next time Carey and I hooked up, he asked if anything had ever happened between Jason and me...a little brotherly rivalry I think. He was relieved to hear nothing had happened, which allowed Carey and me to go back to our usual routine.

Jason disappeared for a while, but I never forgot about him, until he showed up at my house one day, a year or so later—no note, no call, just rang the bell. By this time, I had sworn off Carey, mostly because he only called me when he wanted something...sex, a favor, a question, etc. So Jason and I started hanging out again. It was like no time had passed. Even-tually, I did sleep with Jason, but it was mostly because I thought I'd NEVER go back to my bad habits with Carey. My sex with Jason was the most phenomenal sex I'd had up to that point. He was even more forbid-den than his brother. It's like every time he touched me I'd have an orgasm. The first time we were together I had more orgasms than I could count. That had never happened to me before. I wondered what took me so long to reach this seventh heaven, but I figured it was the forbidden fruit phe-nomenon.

Unfortunately sexual heaven didn't last long. Carey always seemed to show up at my weakest moments. After I had slept with his older brother a few times, he started to call again. One night, he came over, and I realized my Achilles' heel was still there. I still wanted Carey…even though I had just slept with Jason. I was guilt-ridden and didn't know what to do—except to sleep with him. How could I resist, he came over with a bottle of wine, and next thing I knew I was having all night sex with him.

I was now sleeping with brothers. I had conned myself into believing it was OK since I had sworn to never sleep with Jason again. It didn't really matter since Carey and I could never have a real relationship, nor could Jason and I. I was screwed, so I decided to screw them both…literally. To this day, they don't know about each other, but it's been years, you never know, they've probably already swapped stories about me and compared notes. No matter what, I'll always be able to say that I had two very hot, very attractive, very sexually talented brothers. And if I had the chance I'd probably do it all over again, with Carey and Jason or any other brothers out there that I haven't discovered…without the guilt and all the fun. So, Carey and Jason, if you're out there, look me up…you never know, it might not be too creepy after all.

57

FINISHING LAST

A so-called friend of mine, Candy, once told me that if I met a nice guy, I would "just fuck it up." I really do want to fall for a nice guy. And at least I'm trying…unlike some people, judging others and sitting on the sidelines complaining. I may be getting my heart broken every time, but I would rather have that than have my heart and vagina dry up from neglect. A broken heart reminds you that you're still alive and can feel…otherwise I feel like I'm just going through the motions of life.

Candy might have been right, but I must say every man I've ever had a "real" relationship with has been an incredibly nice guy…probably too nice, but that's not their fault. I'm sure that's why those relationships didn't work out. I have the involuntary tendency to push men as much as I can to see what I can get away with. I like getting my way, but if they let me get away with too much I get bored and lose interest. It's a mixed blessing I guess. I'm a daddy's girl. When he was around, I got away with about anything and everything, but I'm like a child, I need discipline and boundaries…if my guy doesn't give them to me, who will?

I can see it now. My personal ad would read something like:

> 29-year-old woman, looking for a man to give boundaries and some good old-fashioned discipline. Enjoys moonlight walks and candlelight dinners.

I'm kidding about the walks and dinners, but it reads like a woman who likes to be dominated. And that's not the case at all. I just want a guy who won't lie like a welcome mat when push comes to shove. A man who can send food back for me when my order isn't right. A man who will stand up for me when my honor, or anything else, is being disgraced. A man with a little assertiveness and strength, someone I can feel protected by. I guess the bottom line is all I want is a guy who I can trust and feel safe with…is that too much to ask for? I don't think so. A man can feel safe with me and if I'm in love with him he can trust me too.

Nice guys are always trying to break character and be the asshole that every woman seems to love. It never works for them; we know when we have a nice guy in our presence…we can smell them a mile away, the way animals can sense fear. Nice guys spend more time trying to be the jerk, that they miss their mark with the ladies. I can't go against my nature and neither should they. Unless the nice guy is SMOKIN' HOT they generally don't stand a chance. The attraction is key to any "relationship" or hook up. That I can guarantee, trust me, I've tried very hard to have sex with men I'm not attracted to just because I'm horny, but it never ever works…meaning no orgasm, no fun.

I'm a nice girl, really I am; a total lady outside of the bedroom, but I'm a total whore once that door shuts…within reason of course. That's all I want, a man who is a gentleman, who's got a backbone, and treats me with a little respect, but a sex-crazed, loyal, adventurous man in bed. Not too unrealistic is it? A nice guy with a good healthy sex drive and technique. I've found that one side-effect of being a nice guy is sexual aptitude. They don't seem to experiment enough or take control of the situation…a little man-handling is good once in a while, but a nice guy wouldn't do that. Maybe that's because they don't get enough practice. They'll have had sex a lot, but not with a large quantity. Nice guys need to play the field and learn about variety, what all girls like and what only some girls want. Practice makes perfect in every aspect of life. If you're a nice guy get out there and practice as much as you can, but if you're unable to get enough girls to volunteer for practice, rent lots of porn. Take notes, and then when you finally find a girl willing, practice everything you've learned on her and see what she likes.

It seems that the asshole wins in the one-night-stand and short term dating arena, whereas the nice guy loses…at least with me. However, the nice guy may not get a lot of random casual sex, but eventually they'll win in the marriage department—whether they like it or not, but only after the good girls hit 35 and get sick of being treated like crap by all the assholes in the world. I guess it's a win-win situation for nice guys and assholes…the asshole probably doesn't want to get married and all the nice guys probably *just* want to get married. Things always seem to have a way of working themselves out in the end.

PART IX

58

THREE'S A CROWD

I've never been in a threesome, but I never really wanted too—at least not with another woman. Don't get me wrong, I'm not morally opposed to them, just not interested in it. I'm just too selfish or insecure to have a threesome, I'm not sure really. It's either that or I just wouldn't want an extra pair of boobs or balls in my face at the drop of a hat, I want to have a little more control of what's happening to me.

I'm needy, I guess that's the bottom line. All the attention has to be on ME. If there's someone else in the room, I might get a little jealous or feel neglected. Not to mention, most men don't know how to handle one woman, let alone two at the same time. If I have to be honest, I wouldn't want to be with a man who wanted to share me…with a man or a woman. I want them to feel like I'm theirs…not possessive or jealous but that sexually it's something that we do together. I know I wouldn't want to see them with another woman and especially not a man, particularly with my taste in men. I'd end up the odd man out.

I'm not into women; I never have been. I've kissed a girl, but that same night I made out with two gay guys at the same time in the boys' bathroom at a gay bar. I would have made out with anyone that night—I can guarantee you that. I don't think there's anything wrong with two girls being together, just like there's nothing wrong with two men being together. Spare me the "it's so beautiful to see two women together" to try and convince me to have a threesome. I've heard it all. Nothing you can say would convince me to be with a woman. I'll only do it if it's my choice. AND I'd choose the woman, because I'm very picky, she'd probably have to be perfect.

I was tempted to be with a woman once. I'll call her Candy. She was a famous porn star. Candy was really beautiful and I knew I wouldn't have to do anything to her and she'd do all the work. I knew she would know exactly what she was doing...if you're going to do it, do it and have it done RIGHT. I said I was tempted, but that wasn't enough motivation for me. With my luck, she would have taped it and I probably would have ended up on some porn shelf someday...a "hidden camera revealed" kind of porn.

My suggestion: go rent porn if you want to see two chicks get it on, instead of trying to convince your girlfriend to do it with you. Or, if you *do* get into a threesome, make sure you don't have any feelings for either of the women involved...just in case it backfires on you. Although, I did date a man who married a woman who loved threesomes. Neal said he just sat back and watched most of the time, and it's one of the main reasons why he married her. Supposedly, he got it out of his system and now doesn't care whether the girl he's with is bisexual or not.

Next time a guy asks to have a threesome, just mention you might just like some boy-on-boy action. It doesn't seem to be a very common female fantasy, but I wonder what you'd do if the tables were turned, and the girl you're with says she wants to see you with a man. I'm not talking about two guys taking on one girl...I'm talking about two guys getting it on without a girl involved! Doesn't seem like a fair trade does it? And I don't know any straight males out there who would be too ready to comply with getting it on with a guy, especially while their girlfriend watched. Tell your guy to think about that before he tries pushing you into it...because if you want to do it, you'll do it. He doesn't need to pressure you or set it up, you can do it all on your own.

All in all, I don't think I would be opposed to two men and me, but I don't know many men who would be comfortable with that either…why the double standard? I asked a guy I know if he'd be up to a threesome with me and another guy. Jason said he'd be ready and willing whenever I give the word, so I'm glad I've got my options open. I might have to set it up…all in the name of research (and pleasure). I'll let you know how it goes.

59

THE A-TEAM AND LESBIANS

M r. T, Murdock, Hannibal, and Face: who didn't love the 80's television show, "The A-Team," that made Mohawks and gold chains a fashion statement? And lesbians! Who doesn't love a good lesbian? Well, maybe not the bull-dyke variety, but there's nothing wrong with a little girl-on-girl action to start your day, especially if they're lipstick lesbians. Although liking and obsessing are two very different things for most people, at least for me. I never thought I would have to combine the two for a good conversation piece with a man. But I shouldn't be surprised about anything when it comes to my dating life.

An older married friend of mine tried setting me up once with, Allen, a guy she worked with. Elaine thought we'd get along fabulously, even if it was just as friends, but she hoped for more. Elaine said she'd have him call me and we'd go out for drinks or something. I met Allen at a bar in my neighborhood and near his work. He was late, I started drinking without him. When he arrived I was pretty sure I wasn't attracted to him, but I thought I wouldn't judge this book by its cover. Allen had a flat face, the kind with no real cheekbones or chin; everything just kind of flowed together with no defining features. I thought if he's a good guy, with a decent personality, that's something I might be able to get over. Allen was English so that helped; he had an accent, which I'm always a sucker for.

After the basic small talk about whom we work for/with and other trivial things, we started talking about what was most important to him: television and chicks. Allen spent most of the evening telling me about his love for that particularly popular 80's television show, "The A-Team". Now, I enjoyed the A-team as much as the next adolescent, but not enough to spend two hours telling anyone the virtues of various episodes, including little known facts, guest star stats, and any other detail Allen could bore me with.

My torture didn't end there. Did I mention that this 31-year-old man collects A-Team figurines AND keeps them in his bedroom? Not that I saw his bedroom, it was another detail that he couldn't hold in about his childhood idols. Allen told me with pride that he owned all the figurines he could find. I didn't even know they made figurines for the A-Team! I don't think it ever crossed his mind that it might be slightly odd for a man in his thirties to be bragging about his doll collection on the first "date."

Like that wasn't bad enough, somehow he made a not-so-subtle segue way into his next favorite topic...LESBIANS. He told me on that month's Playboy, the model was a known lesbian. He told me of his love and obsession with lesbians. His complete and utter fascination with girls on girls. I've been around long enough to know how most men feel about the subject of women being sexual with other women...especially in hopes that the women are friends and "straight" but experimental. I have no problem with this topic. But I do know when a conversation veers from normal to completely obsessive and totally obnoxious. Of course Allen wanted to know if I had ever been with a woman before or if I'd had a threesome. He must have thought that if I had, I'd let him watch. I told him no I hadn't...I think Allen lost interest at that exact moment...like I cared. I just wanted to go home.

Allen was an idiot. He didn't know me that well at that point. It could have been totally offensive to me to talk about girls eating each other out all night, but I don't think he cared much about what I thought. Especially since I just sat there and nodded and did the polite, "oh really!" and "I didn't know that" routine. I was so bored, I almost wished for more Mr. T trivia...almost. Luckily, we both had to work the next day so the night only dragged on for a few hours...I couldn't get out of there fast enough. Obviously I avoided sleeping with this one, barely. I'm sure that if he had ignored me all night, I would have fucked him in the parking lot.

The next day, Allen called me at work. I wasn't surprised, but didn't care. We did know a handful of the same people, so I guess it was the only polite thing to do. Even though we both knew there was absolutely NO chemistry. After the initial chitchat, full of "it was nice to meet you" and crap like that, he got to the point of his call. He asked me if I would go with him to a SWINGERS CLUB! I was completely shocked by this, because not only did I not like him, but we hadn't even kissed. Allen wanted me to basically have sex with him, and then let him watch me have sex with a total stranger or two, while he did the same thing. I have bad taste, but I am very picky in an odd way. I generally have to be remotely attracted to a man I'm having sex with. I may be attracted to them because they're an asshole or a complete moron but it's an attraction nonetheless.

Apparently, the night before I'd casually said "I'll try about anything once, within reason." It appears that by this statement Allen assumed that I'd be up for absolutely *anything*...sexually and otherwise. I told Allen that I didn't think I'd be up for something like that, at least not with him. It would be one thing if someone I had an existing sexual relationship with asked me to go, but I didn't want to sleep with Allen, let alone watch him have sex. ICK! Allen then asked me if I could hook him up with a club, since I told him I had a friend who went to swinger's clubs and he didn't begin to know how to find such a "club." I told him I'd look into it just to get him off the phone and out of my life for good.

I never talked to Allen again after that, but I made sure that I told all of his friends and co-workers what I knew. They all thought it was quite weird, but there were a couple who weren't surprised. They didn't know Allen had that sort of side to him, but they probably also didn't know of his fetish for lesbians and the A-Team. Now they do! If I wanted to go to a swingers club I'd pick the guy I was going with, someone I wanted to have sex with at the very least. If I'm interested in a swingers club someday...I'll let you all know when I'm ready. I'm sure it'll be fascinating or traumatizing at the very least.

60

SWINGERS

O pen relationships, group sex, and voyeurism—what more could an easy girl with bad taste want? Well, I don't think it's for me…at times I wish it were, but it's just not. I have to be attracted to the person I'm having sex with, even if it's a beer-goggle attraction. I can imagine a swingers club would work something like this:

Me: "Hi, I'm Angel."

Him: "I'm Ralph."

Me: "So, top or bottom? Missionary or doggie?"

Him: "It's up to you."

Me: "Okay."

After that brief get-to-know-you stage, straight into the action…no conversation or foreplay. Just "Hello," and "How do you wanna fuck?" I'm old-fashioned, I like to know a guy for at least a few hours before I see him naked…or before he sees me naked. What's wrong with wanting to know a little more than just circumcised or not before we fuck? I know that's not how it really works, but that's the visual I have in my head.

I dated a reformed swinger once. Richard left that life behind him in hopes of a more "normal" personal life. I was his guinea pig. For some odd reason he started with me, someone who isn't so normal...at least personality wise, but I guess sexually I am normal and boring, compared to him. I think I drove Richard back to that lifestyle...I couldn't live up. Going from group sex to monogamy can be pretty tedious and tiresome no matter how great the sex is. One-on-one can be boring for anyone, even if they don't have the orgies and variety to compare it too.

What I don't understand is that if men know that ninety-nine percent of all women can't detach sex from emotion, then why would you ever want to allow them to have sex with other men, let alone, in front of you? I can detach myself in a one-night stand, but not sex with the same man on a regular basis. Even if I could fully detach from the sex, I think that I, personally, would also become detached from the man I was in a relationship with. And, if I actually decided to venture into the swinger life style it would only mean that I'm bored with my existing sex life. But that's just me.

I've done the research, on a book level, and it brings some couples closer— it's more honest. So, honestly, it probably wouldn't work for me. There are obviously many people out there who can successfully live the swinger lifestyle and maintain a healthy relationship, but I don't think I'm one of them. Why on earth any man would allow me to have sex with another man is beyond my comprehension. I'd probably be in a relationship, do the swinger thing and fall out of love with my man and into love or lust with the man I was fucking. Why risk it just for variety and momentary gratification?

Along with all of my other quirks, I totally have hygiene issues. I could never be with a man or woman who isn't super clean and who doesn't believe in bathing very often. I know I'd shower right before going to a swingers club but I don't know that everyone else will. Not everybody is that conscious of their hygiene. And, even if they do shower it doesn't mean that all of their parts that really need to be cleaned get sufficiently scrubbed until it's decontaminated and de-polluted and de-kootified. I would have to suggest a group shower, then a good old-fashioned de-lousing and manual inspection. Hygiene also includes grooming. Grooming is very important: trimming, shaving, and cleanliness. These things are good. There things that are not good: super hairy, untrimmed, and dirty. The last thing I would want is to have some big hairy dirty thing coming at me...and I would assume you're lying if you said any different, unless of course you have a dirty, hairy fetish, then that may be your dream come true.

I wouldn't want to be doing my thing and then have some guy, or worse yet some girl, doing whatever they felt like to me while I was busy doing my thing. Even if saying "no thank you" is acceptable, I'm not good at that. Maybe it's the control freak in me that wants to always know what's going on. Or maybe it's just that I like only men one at a time. At times I wish I wasn't like that. Sometimes I wish I were more willing to try something crazy, but I really have no desire to be crazier than I already am AND I really don't feel like getting kooties from some dude I wouldn't normally talk to, let alone have him shove his penis somewhere it doesn't belong. On top of my other obvious issues, I need to concentrate when I'm having sex…I have A.D.D., I'm distracted very easily. If I lose my concentration I lose my orgasm…and that isn't a good thing.

So, no matter how many swinger offers I get, I'll be declining for now. I'm open to it down the road, but it will be a very long road and if that road ends, the swinging will be done *when* I want and *how* I want. There is no other way I'd have it!

61

PEEPING TOM

Voyeur? Pervert? Peeping tom? I like to watch people having sex live and in front of me. Unfortunately I haven't had the opportunity too often, but I think that's been more of a choice than lack of opportunity. I've been on a few porn sets, which allowed me to watch professionals do it up close and personal; that was fun and a big turn on. I would highly suggest attending a shoot to anyone who ever gets the rare opportunity.

I don't want to watch just *anybody* have sex. On the set, they were pretty people and I knew that going in. If I had to watch a bunch of people who look like my aunt and uncle having sex, it would really make me queasy. I've never really went looking for live sex action, maybe because of that reason…also I really don't know where to look for hot looking couples willing to have sex in front of an audience. I guess I might if I knew they were porn stars or extremely capable at their tasks at hand. One of my boyfriends, Chuck, woke me up one night to have the following conversation:

Chuck: Honey, wake up.

Me: *(groggy)* What's going on?

      I thought maybe he was drunk or something and wanted to have sex.

Chuck: I was wondering if you wanted to go to a swingers club next weekend with me?

Me: *(my reflex response)* No, now let me sleep.

Chuck: Let me finish…not to have sex, just to watch people have sex.

Me: Um, no. I just watched a special on HBO about swingers clubs…and I really don't want to watch ugly people have sex. I'm sorry, baby.

Chuck: I don't like watching ugly people either, but they won't be ugly.

Me: You can't guarantee that.

He looked disappointed.

Me: I'm not saying no forever, I just don't think I'm comfortable with it right now.

He was satisfied with that and I went back to sleep.

I would have to request headshots, and complete nude shots of all the people attending, before I could consent to going to a swinger's party, because, unfortunately, in reality not everyone looks like they belong on TV. I am so picky that I think when it came down to it I'd end up picking no one. There's nothing wrong with being picky in your voyeurism. Be picky, I highly suggest it. If you don't want to see fat people doing it, choose not to…it's not my fault I'm a snob. You can be one too if you really want to.

I'd rather watch a great well-groomed man with a hot bod and a large dick fuck the shit out of a beautiful woman with real boobs and a nice body. That's why I watch porn. That's why I'm picky about the porn I watch, no amateur videos, no caught on tape, just good old-fashioned well-lit porn with beautiful people. I don't think that's too much to ask. The odds are if I ever did go to a pretty swingers club, I'd get turned on and want to do it…the problem would then be that I'd be having sex and would then be the person on display and someone might be saying I'm not attractive enough either…I don't want that!

I'm not much of an exhibitionist. I don't like being watched or stared at, so even if it were a situation where that happened, I'd be so self-conscious that

I don't think I could actually enjoy the sex. I guess I'm screwed either way, being watched or being the watcher. I suppose I'll have to stick to my boring, one-on-one private action until I find a way to get my nerve up to be more public.

62

HOME MOVIES

Women in society are not supposed to enjoy, watch, or own pornography, and if you do, it's a dirty little secret you're supposed to keep to yourself. Well, I've got a few dirty little secrets of my own and I love them. I get one out whenever I'm horny and alone, or not alone as the case is generally.

I'm not afraid to admit that I like porn, but not all types. Most porn is definitely geared toward men and it's not fair. If the people who produce porn geared their product toward the straight female persuasion, we'd buy more. It would be more accepted and men wouldn't have to twist their girlfriend's arm to watch it once in awhile. Most women want good porn with a good story, good acting, pretty people, and great sex...we'd be lined up in droves to buy it. I would, even though that scenario is pretty unrealistic.

I used to produce a radio show that had porn stars as guests. My staff and I actually went to a porn set and distribution center as part of a segment. It was really cool watching a gorgeous woman with large breasts and a really hot young guy with a big dick have sex for a couple of hours! And we got lots of free porn to take home. It was a fun day. It's the only profession I know of where the men work harder than the women and get paid less. I actually felt sorry for the guy. He wasn't allowed to cum for hours. First, he couldn't hold it then he couldn't maintain an erection. Fortunately for him, I think he enjoyed it. It looked like "hard" but fun work, with a climatic reward and a decent paycheck. Afterwards, all I wanted was to go home and get laid. Unfortunately, I didn't that day because I had to go back to work, but it's a nice memory to think about.

I actually got my favorite porn from working on that show; we "reviewed" porn for our listeners so we'd get more free porn from producers. My favorite has no story, no dialogue, no acting, just sex! The locale, positions, and partners change, but the bottom line is its just sex...with very attractive people. I'd rather have just the sex scenes than distracting dumb dialogue and horrendous acting. We all know they're going to get it on, they should just do it. Especially since we're not going to get the Oscar winning story...we might as well have the action.

I am a little ashamed to say that I have some more personal experience in the movie making experience on the amateur level. When I was in college, I was dating a guy who lived across the courtyard from my apartment. Tyler and I were together all the time. We were both sophomores and we had been dating for about nine months, so it was still a little exciting and new, but old enough that we looked for "adventure."

During Christmas break we had his apartment to ourselves. All the roommates had gone home and we wanted to stick around and have some fun. We decided to do something neither of us had ever tried—taping ourselves having sex and other activities. He held the camera while I gave him a BJ. That was quite unflattering for me. I didn't like watching it either. Back then I really hated the way I looked and really didn't want to see myself on camera. I know it's silly now that I think about it, but I was only nineteen years old. We also set up a tripod so we could record us having sex...that was fun and I was actually more comfortable with that.

Each time we watched something we'd recorded, I made my boyfriend erase it or tape over it; I didn't want any evidence of our "bad" behavior. It was pleasurable and entertaining, but after a few times the thrill was gone. We'd been there, done that. I'm sure I would have enjoyed it a lot more if I'd been able to watch our handiwork without wanting to cover my eyes and go on a diet. I think that if I were to record myself now it would be a lot different. I'd make sure the lighting was better. Unfortunately, it's too easy nowadays for some guy to put that crap on the Internet or something; it would have to be with a boyfriend and not a fling and I would have to have complete control over the footage to protect it from falling into the wrong hands AND so I could show my friends. Kidding.

A few weeks later, when school was back in session, my father came to visit, which was very rare. He stopped by since he was in the area. He mentioned that he needed his video camera back. I told him okay and sent Tyler to go get it. While we visited, my dad told me he didn't have any blank VHS tapes so I offered up one of my blank tapes. I figured it was the least I could do since he loaned me the camera.

A couple of weeks went by when I got a phone call from my dad and the conversation went a little like this:

> DAD: Angel!
>
> ME: Yeah dad!
>
> *I knew I was in trouble by his tone, I just didn't know what for.*
>
> DAD: You have to promise me you'll NEVER EVER DO THAT AGAIN.
>
> *I immediately knew exactly what he meant. I had not given my father a blank tape like I thought, but the tape that my boyfriend and I had been using. MY FATHER SAW THE TAPE! I was mortified, but all I could say was:*
>
> ME: Okay dad.
>
> DAD: Because you never know who might see it! (*Obviously!!!!*)

The conversation ended there. Tyler couldn't look my father in the eyes for a long time. I couldn't either; my dad is a scary-protective-southern-ex-military type who would kill anyone who hurt me, or worse yet, kill ME for doing something so stupid. To this day my father is a little too protective, but once a daddy's girl always a daddy's girl and I would be overly protective too if I had guys putting my daughter on tape.

Hopefully, Dad will never see any of the photos of me that are floating around from my college days either. They're embarrassing and unflattering and I look ugly and fat. In my defense, I should tell you that they are the "artsy kind" but that's still no excuse. I figure it this way, if they ever surface anywhere other than on my own wall, it could only help my insufficient and inadequate career, or at least get me a pity date or two. If Playboy would come my way, I would gladly accept so I could redeem myself in the pages of their beautiful magazine.

So, the moral of the story: If you're going to tape yourself having sex with someone, be bright enough not to borrow your father's camera and then give him back the tape. Fork out the dough and buy your own camera with a remote control. Unless you're an exhibitionist too, then just find someone to film it for you—just make sure you have the *only* copy.

PART X

63

CRUCIFIED

*I*nnocent until proven guilty? Never in my case. I have always been judged and sentenced before I even know I'm being accused of anything. I don't know if it's because of the way I look or the way I act or that people assume once an adulterer always an adulterer or once a whore always a whore. No matter the case, I have been unjustly crucified for actions I have not taken. It forces me to do the only thing I can do after serving my time as an innocent victim: I do whatever it was that I was accused of. If I'm going to do the time, I might as well do the crime.

Since I grew up in a small town where everyone knew everybody's business, or at least they thought they knew everybody's business, it was very hard to keep anything private. It sucked. Back then, I hated having people know my business, talking behind my back. I still do, but now I'll willingly tell you my business in black and white. I, however, am giving you the truth and not just rumor and gossip and it's on my terms. The only way I like it.

Also, being raised in a small town didn't allow much job opportunity, so I earned my college money by working as a truck driver on a farm. I did this every summer from the day I got my driver's license until I graduated from college. It paid fairly well and I didn't have to work all summer in a boring job. Generally, I was the only girl on a farm within a 20-mile radius so it was pretty fun. One summer, before I even arrived back in town from college, I heard rumors that I was sleeping with my new and married boss. I wasn't sure how I would have accomplished that, since I hadn't been in town since the summer before. Maybe a long distance affair? I think my old boss started the rumor, jealous I wasn't working for him.

It was really silly, but it started becoming an annoyance. Conversations would stop when I walked into the ONE grocery store (if you could call it that) in town. I always knew they were talking about me, but generally it was based in a little truth and not a complete lie. Then, my boss started getting harassed by his wife and farm partners, telling him to stop fooling around with me when we hadn't done anything. We were attracted to each other and were flirting, but we weren't crossing any lines. We were innocent, but no one believed us.

His wife hated me before she even met me. It isn't an uncommon thing for women to hate me for no reason, but she had no real reason to feel that way. It was her fault that she believed the gossip more than she believed her own husband. According to him, he'd never really had an affair.

Finally, after a night of drinking after work, we talked about how stupid it was that we were essentially getting punished for doing nothing. I was definitely getting the lesser end of the punishment stick. I only had to deal with the rumors, and to be honest, I was used to it. We decided that if we were going to be in trouble anyway, we might as well DO what we were in trouble for.

One night, we got drunk and fooled around. It was great, except for the fact that I had a real crush on the guy. My emotions were already involved, and I think that his were too. We were friends first and since we didn't have sex immediately the emotions grew. That made it even worse because by the time we did have sex on his bathroom floor, it was more than a fling. I didn't have any guilt for this one, though. I think I was feeling more guilt before we got involved, because I was accused of wrong doing beforehand it made it much easier to cross those boss-employee and adulterer lines.

I always thought it was funny that if no one had accused of us having sex and hadn't gossiped about it nonstop, we probably never would have done it. I never would have had one of the most fun-filled working summers of my life. Having something more to look forward to at work than just work sure does make it easier to wake up in the morning. We'd fool around before work. We'd fool around after work. We'd fool around during work.

It was great. And for me it was definitely not based on sex, because we only had sex a couple of times.

Toward the end of the affair, he asked me what I wanted for my birthday. I told him that all I wanted was to stay the night with him in his house—a fitting end to a mad love affair. He said he would do what he could. I look back on this request and realize how stupid and selfish it was, but the first chance we had to do this we did. We had sex in his shower. We had sex on the floor. We had sex in his bedroom. It was kind of romantic and sick all at the same time. Waking up in another woman's bed is a little unsettling, but I was happy I got what I wanted for my birthday.

I have always felt it was more of a love affair than a plain old affair, even though I knew we wouldn't see each other again after the job ended. After the summer ended, I never saw him again. It was over. I went back to school. I knew it would never last past September and I was okay with that. He was entrenched in his farm, family, and life. I'm sure some day I'll run into him, if I ever go back to my hometown again, but that could be twenty years from now. He'll still be with his wife. He'll still be a farmer, wanting more out of life than farming. He'll probably still be the gossip of the town, unless another scandalous affair finally replaced us in the stupid gossip mill of that little town.

That was my last real affair with a married man. I'm not saying I haven't hooked up with any after that, but it has always been of the one-time variety. It's weird, nowadays the first thing I look at is a guy's ring finger, an attempt to ward off or prevent any attraction to a married man. It's just that I don't think I could get involved with one again, especially one who is my boss. Not only did it make work a little difficult, trying to keep it a secret and not actually getting caught. But I have to admit I was a little heartbroken when the summer ended. He was a really cool guy, minus the cheating on his wife thing.

I think about him once in awhile, but more because I feel sorry for him. I know he's not happy with his life. I know that that summer affair was probably the most exciting thing to have happened to him in that town…hopefully he's found other ways to add excitement to his humdrum life. Maybe I will have to go back "home" and pay him a visit…I think he'd enjoy that. Maybe. It would give all those bored housewives and farmers something to talk about, that's for sure.

64

HARD AT WORK

*E*ven though while growing up, I was always a big-town girl trapped in a small town, I lacked the real big-town experience. Excluding hanging out in Seattle whenever I had the chance and going to New York City as a kid, I had never really been exposed to city living. At least not on my own and not as an adult, and because of that I arrived in Los Angeles with my small town ideals and my trusting nature in overdrive.

I got my first interview within a couple of days; a college alumni helped set it up for me. The position was in business affairs at an advertising agency that had it's own production department. It would have been a great first job and I was lucky to get the interview, especially since the only thing I had lined up was an unpaid internship with a movie producer and my funds were quickly running dry. I was desperate. I think people in L.A. can smell desperation like animals can smell fear, and they take that information and use it to their advantage.

I made an appointment with the Vice President, the friend of a friend who facilitated the interview, with Jerry, the business affairs guy, late forties, if not late fifties, balding, you know the type. The first interview with Jerry went well. He said we'd need to meet again and wanted to know if we could do the interview at drinks, instead of the office. His explanation was that the person being replaced didn't know yet and so the whole interview process needed to be "covert."

I was so new to the interview game that I didn't know whether or not that was normal, so we went to drinks at the Four Seasons, which happened to be across the street from his new apartment. Jerry disclosed that he was in the middle of a divorce and was now living alone. The continuation of the interview seemed more personal than professional at this point, but I thought he was just being friendly, helping a new girl in town with all sorts of information...where to live, where to go, etc. etc. I was grateful at first...he even mentioned there was an open studio in his building, since I had no place to live at that point. He also recommended where I could purchase a good and inexpensive sleeper couch since I had no furniture for when I did have a place to live.

At this point I was thinking the "interview" was going quite well. Jerry then mentioned that I should take a look at his building and his new couch, which was just across the street. It seemed like a natural thing to do at the time and I thought that since he was old enough to be my father that it was purely paternal on his part. God I was naïve and I went willingly!

I went up to Jerry's apartment and he soon expressed his interest in me— as an employee AND as a possible date. He told me that he would leave it up to me on both counts. I didn't know what to say...I was in desperate need for a job, but was not willing to go *that* far for one. Even though he said one had nothing to do with the other, I knew better. I told Jerry I would think about it, thanked him and got out of there as soon as I could. I couldn't believe that a potentially career-making or at least rent-paying job had been ruined.

Jerry called to officially offer me the job soon after that, but I had already made up my mind that I couldn't work in that kind of environment. How stupid would I be to have my first job with and work directly under a man I wasn't attracted to, but who'd expressed his intentions? I had the first panic attack of my life. Not only was the guy unattractive, he just gave me the creeps. I was about to give up on the whole regular job thing. I was thinking seriously about the "exotic dancer" profession...at least until I made that first big deal, got noticed as a writer or whatever it was that I wanted to do—to pay the bills. I was desperate. I was scared.

A few months later, I ran into Jerry at a bookstore. I politely said hello then went on my way. It didn't take long for me to realize that he was following

me around the store. It was really weird. I knew that I made the right decision in not working for him, obviously. It would have been a nightmare.
From then on, I've always avoided those kinds of working environments
from the beginning, especially when I know it'll go badly from the beginning. That's part of my problem though, I never know it's going to go
badly from the beginning. I just got lucky that one time…maybe that
should be one of *my* interview questions: "And do you plan on hitting on
me now or anytime in the future?" Make it clear from the get-go. That
would probably insure that I'd never get another job again…oh well…back
to the drawing board.

65

DOWN THE CORPORATE COCK

S ome women have mastered the art of sleeping their way up the corporate ladder. This is something that I have not been able to grasp. Whenever I have slept with a boss or with someone of authority, it has only hurt my career. On the flip side, I *have* mastered the much more difficult and less rewarding method of sleeping my way down the ladder.

During my self-discovering career path, I got bored with massage therapy and attempted to return to the mainstream and torturous entertainment business. A friend of mine got me a job working at a dot.com radio station. It was going to be fun, because it was one of those laidback environments: shorts, khakis, dogs welcome, and drinking on the job. However, now that I look back, it was just STUPID. Forty and fifty year olds running around in Bermuda shorts and t-shirts on scooters indoors and acting like kids. They really didn't present images of respect and reliability, which is proba-bly why they wasted 30 million dollars in 18 months, most of which, I would guess, went into the CEO's pocket.

Anyhow, the minute I started working there, my co-workers began to tell me that the millionaire CEO, Shelly had "yellow-fever," meaning he

LOVED Asians, and would just "love" me. And Shelly did start checking me out immediately. He was troll-ish and hairy and short with big feet (the myth is NOT true...big feet only mean big shoes). At a company party, Shelly expressed his interest in me by telling me that he'd have to fire me to date me! Classy wasn't he?

After that night, everyone in the company assumed I had slept with Shelly when I hadn't! Not that I blame them much. I did pass out at the party at his house after he gave me a Vicodin with an alcohol chaser. In addition, it didn't help that I was walking through my hotel lobby in leather pants, same party shirt, and wet hair with him the next morning. My humiliated parade through the lobby didn't really create a prudish or celibate image of me to my new co-workers. I'd only been employed for about a week at that point. I would have thought the same thing.

Shelly began calling me almost every night and day from that point on...emailing, flirting, getting jealous. It was very odd but we were becoming "friends." If I were his friend, though, I would hate to see how he trashed his enemies. I guess through this so-called friendship I started to see past the hairy back and troll-ish appearance to become attracted to his true personality. A big old-fashioned asshole. But I think I've demonstrated repeatedly that I like assholes, so there's nothing new with that scenario. You asshole...me likey! Simple isn't it?

I did end up sleeping with Shelly about six months later. Again, everyone believed we already had before we really did, but I only did it this time because I was drunk as shit and hadn't had sex in a few months. Didn't feel it, don't remember it. Just the way I like it with him. Shelly's on my top ten list of bad in bed—not because I'm being spiteful, but because he was BAD. He boasted otherwise, but I can honestly say, he's wrong and I'm RIGHT! As usual.

The sexual relationship didn't last long because it was bad sex and the "challenge" for him was over. The funny thing is anyone who knows me knows that I am NOT a challenge. Either way, Shelly made sure everyone in the company knew what had happened and then some, even though he made *me* swear not to tell ANYONE. He said it would affect my job and his if anyone knew. Apparently he just wanted the "glory" of being the first to tell and tell whatever he wanted. I was oblivious to this fact. I thought our secret was safe. Even though it had been assumed for months, I didn't want everyone in the company to definitely know.

He should have just announced it on the radio. Fewer people would have known and it wouldn't have hurt my career as much. I should have listened to everyone and sued Shelly's ass for slander or whatever the legal statute would be. I'm not that kind of girl. I've been the receiver of welcomed and un-welcomed harassment from the minute I was capable of holding down a job, so I've gotten used to it.

After my horrible sexual experience was over with the CEO, I began to take notice of the new Vice President. He was hot in a surfer boy sort of way and it didn't take long for James to take notice of me. In hindsight, I don't know if he took notice of me for me or for the graphic details the CEO was sharing. I guess it didn't really matter at the time. We still went out a few times and fooled around a tiny bit.

It was a lot of fun until my co-workers began to gossip again. They were impressed with my ability to sleep my way *down* the ladder. Lucky for me, the company went bankrupt soon thereafter. I never did sleep with James, nor did I ever see Shelly again except for his drive-bys past my house. That really creeped me out, but what is a girl supposed to do? And I did receive a threatening phone call from him telling me to not contact a lawyer regarding our "consensual" sex. Apparently, I wasn't the only person he'd been sleeping with and a few of the others had contacted their attorneys, just like I should have but didn't. I told Shelly that if he'd leave me alone I'd leave the lawyers out of it; he left me alone after that.

The moral of the story, if there is one is: If you're going to sleep with the boss, try to get more out of it than a bad reputation. Try to get a raise at least for Christ's sake! And then don't date the other help! Otherwise, don't waste your time with a co-worker or boss. It's just an unpleasant situation all around. Don't do it. If you've never done it, you'll just have to trust me.

PART XI

66

LUCKY DOG

I am a lucky bitch. I've never been attacked, kidnapped, or raped even though I've put myself into some potentially dangerous situations. I'm less naïve now, I hope, but a few years ago that wasn't the case. I hope my good luck and fortune continues. Even if my luck hasn't brought me a good man, it hasn't brought much emotional or physical scarring.

When I first moved to Los Angeles seven years ago, I didn't know a soul. I'd been to LA once, five years earlier, but only for a couple days and purely did the touristy thing. Before I moved, one of my guy friends, who I never slept, told me he had a house. Actually, I think he said "a mansion" in LA that a friend was staying in and that I could too. He was saving my life. I could stay for a few months until I found a job and my own place. The pressure was off.

Before I left Washington, my friend made the arrangements and instructed me to call Mack when I was almost there. I hadn't spoken to Mack yet, but trusted everything was cool. When I arrived at the outskirts of LA I finally got a hold of Mack. I was exhausted and excited to see my new, temporary home. At this time, I discovered that the house wasn't exactly *in* Los Angeles, but almost 50 miles away. That's a long way from anywhere, but for Los Angeles, it might as well have been 400 miles. I also discovered that the mansion wasn't exactly a mansion, but an apartment. As if that wasn't bad enough, I learned that I wouldn't have my own room because it was a one-bedroom apartment. I freaked. I wasn't sure if my so-called friend was trying to pimp me out or what, but I didn't know what to do. I didn't know anyone, nor did I have much money.

Lucky for me, Mack couldn't have been nicer. He let me take over his bedroom and he slept on the couch for a full month. He never made a move on me and we even talked about getting a two-bedroom apartment in Los Angeles together, which didn't happen but he was nice nonetheless. I never did speak to my "friend" back home again. Hmmm...Maybe I should call him and invite him to stay in my "mansion" on the beach!

Unfortunately, my stupidity did not stop there. While looking for a place to live I drove all over Los Angeles. I got lost more times than I would want to remember and I had a reality check about how much it would really cost to live in sunny California—especially since I didn't have a job and barely had enough money to get an apartment, which I had to borrow from my mom. Not only that, but I learned I would have to actually have a job and/or some sort of income to get an apartment. I was so green. I thought being a nice person with a college degree would be good enough to pass a credit check.

One day while I was at a payphone, a guy pulled up, I began to walk away when I heard him say hello. I said hello. I'm from a small town; everyone talks to everyone...we're friendly that way. I told him I was new in town and looking for an apartment. He grew up in L.A. and said he'd help me look for an apartment, since I didn't know the hood from a hole in the wall. I thought that was very sweet...a complete stranger offering to help a new girl in town.

The next day he called. We met at Big Bob's restaurant. I parked my car, got into his and Julian started driving me around good neighborhoods I could afford. Nobody knew me, where I was, who I was with, nothing. You always hear of girls getting abducted and killed. I could have been one of them and no one would have noticed. We ended up driving by an apartment that I fell in love with. I applied, and paid for the credit check. Julian owned his own business and said that I could put him down as an employer. Without him I wouldn't have gotten the apartment, an apartment that I still live in to this day. I was grateful...but unfortunately for Julian, not that grateful.

We ended up back at his place in the hills. I think he considered it a "closer." We hung out, ate, talked, but I was exhausted and ready to go back to my car, for my 50-mile drive "home." Julian stopped me for a moment to kiss me, and then asked me if he could seduce me. I was surprised and grateful he had asked. But I said no. I don't think he thought I was grateful enough or appreciative enough for all he had done for me. Again, lucky for me, Julian couldn't have been more of a gentleman. Well, he tried a little more, but he basically took "no" for what it meant this time, NO!

Not necessarily good judgment, just pure undeniable luck. Because I've made so many bad decisions and had lapses in judgment, I do believe that something is keeping me safe. It might be luck or a universal force or a guardian angel or karma or some mystical being. Whatever it is, I'm grateful because I can be such an idiot. I'm much more skeptical now…possibly too much, but I think it's keeping me a little more safe than I was when I first arrived in Hollywood.

I just hope someday this "thing" that is keeping me safe brings me a good man who I can fall in love with. Until then, I'll have to be satisfied with it keeping me from harms way since I, obviously, am an idiot! I no longer rely on this unseen force, but I'm thankful it was there when I needed it. Now I use my best judgment, which isn't great, but it's better than using none at all.

67

MADONNA WHORE

I have been the object of many a man with the Madonna Whore complex. I, of course, would be the whore in the equation. I don't mind that, though. The Madonnas never get much sex, just the love. Not that I don't want love, but sex is much more tangible. I have come to believe that like so many men out there, I too have my own version of this "disorder." I don't think I can have a healthy hot sex life with a man I'm in a relationship with, nor can I fall in real love with a man I have great sex with. And it sucks! Why can't I be normal? Really, why can't I?

Men aren't the only ones with commitment issues. I'm thinking of starting a support group for commitment phobic women. That way we don't feel like outcasts and so lonely when our mothers and sisters ask us why we're not married or in a relationship of some sort. There's nothing wrong with not being with someone or wanting to be with someone. I do realize that I have issues that aren't normal. However, no matter what my issues may or may not be, I shouldn't be judged on my relationship status or lack thereof by everyone in a relationship—probably an unhappy one at that.

I used to not understand how some men could view women for two different purposes: the wife or mother and the whore. Unable to love someone you've got great sex with but love someone in an almost platonic nature, since it is without the sexual aspect of a "real" relationship. I did say, used to, because I have realized that I have lust for those who could never be a husband or boyfriend to me, but the men that I had and have good relationships with, I do not like having sex with. I swear I had to have been a man in my last life or just a very butch woman…not a lesbian, but close. Or possibly a butch gay guy, since I love men so much. Either way, something screwed me up…a lot!

There's got to be a new term for someone like me…or maybe it's just because I probably have a split personality or something easily defined as that. One personality that doesn't want a relationship of any kind…the other, less dominate personality, wanting a relationship and a man more than anything else. I think everyone has some aspects of this disorder…more pronounced in some, less in others. I'm not so abnormal after all, I just happen to know myself really well and know what my different personalities want. And I figure it this way, eventually the personality that wants a relationship will win out. Not necessarily out of want, but more out of need. I assume eventually I'll get tired of sleeping around and, as I get older, it will be harder to attract and find men good enough to sleep with. I don't want to be that over-the-hill chick still trying to live the single life. So, while I'm young I need to find a guy who's decent enough to be with on a more permanent basis. I'll become the Madonna of the equation…being loved but not getting any sex. Hey, I can't wait to get what I want…yeah, right!

Have you ever seen that movie, SINGLES? It was a 1990's movie about a bunch of single apartments with single people trying to find love, starring Bridget Fonda and Matt Dillon. Bridget's character is asked what she wants in a man, she says that at first she wanted the perfect guy and she explains how long her list of characteristic was. She then says she learned through trial and error that those things weren't reasonable or possible so she narrowed it down to a man who says, "Bless you!" when she sneezes. Pretty basic, but it says so much about men who do such simple and courteous things without thinking…and it illustrates how we lower our standards so much when we want a man to love us.

Through my own trial and error I've learned these things about myself and what I want out of my prospective mate: I'm easy. I am odd. I am honest. I am weird. I am needy. I am emotionally, but not physically, high-maintenance, except for lots of sex. I don't need a guy to drive a nice car, take me to fancy restaurants, have a great job; I wouldn't mind, but I don't need these things. It's not like I have unreasonable expectations for the man of my dreams. I want a man to be nice to me…which is a very common want for a lot of women, especially after a little time has passed, but getting a guy to be nice and not TOO nice is where the difficulty lies. I'm not talking about being nice to us to get us in bed, but if you actually want to see us and be with us, we want you to be NICE.

However, I also have to admit that I am attracted to power, drive, ambition, confidence, etcetera, and those characteristics, at times, accompany successful men with money. These qualities also seem to be possessed by total and complete dick-head jerks; that's a bad taste hurdle I'm still trying to get over. On the flip side, I am also attracted to the artistic dreamers who are usually poor as dirt and I end up paying for dinner, but they've got that tortured soul that I love so much, just like mine.

I want a man to care about me. I want a man to need me as much as I need him. I want a fairly tall, dark-haired man with a strong sex drive and who knows what to do with it, but a romantic at heart. Honest to the bone. Genuine. And most of all, I just want to be loved…passionately…is that so much to ask for? Probably. Most definitely. Absolutely.

Those are my wants and needs, in a nutshell. Now that I see them all written out, maybe they are a little unattainable in ONE man…maybe that's why I can't find only ONE man to satisfy my needs. But what I want and hope for, and what I expect to get are two totally different things. I expect to not get a man with all of my wants. I expect to be single for a very long time. I expect that I'll have to have sex with a lot of frogs before I find someone who isn't such a frog. I guess the bottom line is that if I had to pick one thing, or if I hope to get one or two traits in my man it would be: I just want a man who I want to sleep with to be nice to me. Then go from there. Simple. Basic. Realistic. Achievable. Not too bad for a total nut-job, right? Maybe I'm not a lost cause after all?

68

SCAREDY CAT, SCAREDY CAT

*I*f you haven't figured it out yet, I'm a big fat scaredy cat. I am deathly afraid of falling in love. I'm afraid of needing someone and depending on someone to the point of being paralyzed. I'm just scared. I think a lot of people are when it comes to relationships, but some people don't let it get in the way. I really am trying, but I don't think I'm doing so well. The minute I need someone, I run. The minute I have to rely on someone, I freak.

I think there are more of us running from relationships because of fear than not. We probably just disguise it in other ways and don't admit the real root of the problem, going from one short-term relationship to another. I know I have trust issues. I know that I have an irrational fear of all things relationship related. I am working on it, but every time I meet someone I like, I think, "Is this my horrible bad taste at work again?" "Is this another commitment phobic man in disguise?" I second-guess every feeling, every action, and every ounce of hope that it might work out, that I might be happy with someone someday.

What if I were to fall in love? I don't think I've ever really been IN love, I've loved before but there's a difference. I digress…so, what if I fall in love, trust someone, get to need and rely on someone and then they turn into my worst nightmare? Or I turn into my worst nightmare…a fat, unattractive, old nag type who just bitches non-stop at her husband or boyfriend? I think I've been there before and don't want to go back. The second-guessing is unproductive and negative, but it's all a part of my arsenal in my defense mechanism. It's worked pretty well so far. My walls are thick. My walls are high. It will be a challenge for any man who hopes to really get through them. Good luck to anyone who tries with someone like me because you'll really need it. A pound of luck and a lot of fucking patience.

I am worse than any guy I've ever dated and that's really hard for me to admit. If someone great comes along whom I'm actually attracted to and appears to actually care about me and wants to be with me, I can think of a thousand reasons to either sabotage it before I get too close or just run for the hills. I tell them I don't want a relationship, even if deep down I think it will work out. In those instances, I go out of my way to let them know I'm not looking for Mr. Right, never admitting to them that I actually believe we could be the happy couple who lives happily ever after in my head. Instead, I tell them I'm OK with just sex or nothing with them, avoiding any chance of an actual relationship.

The voice inside my head tells me, in reality shouts at me, to "RUN! RUN FOR THE HILLS! GET OUT WHILE YOU STILL CAN!" That voice is deafening. I go out of my way to tell men what's going on in my head. My secret desire is for them to see through the façade and know that it means, "I really like you and I'm afraid." The last guy I told about the voice told me I couldn't run away from him. He wouldn't let me. But maybe that's because he was waiting for the guys with the straight jackets to come and take me away from him.

That's, in all probability, how to get me into a real relationship: persistence and not listening. But possibly, it's not. The last "boyfriend" I had convinced me to be in a relationship with him…telling me how much he loved me and wouldn't hurt me. Three months in he told me he wasn't ready for a relationship. It's the destroy, conquer, and leave-the-rubble-behind technique. I have used it at times, but try not to use my powers on the innocent bystander, just for the losers I attract.

I sometimes think I'm totally full of crap in general, in the sense that the romantic in me would love to meet a great guy, fall in love, have him propose with a huge rock from Tiffany's or Harry Winston's, in the most romantic way ever, get married, eloping of course, and then live happily ever after. But the realist in me knows better and really, what are the odds of that ever happening to me? So, I guess I'll have to continue to hope that some of the crappy relationships or guys I get involved with might actually work out someday.

I've always wondered if there is a "Happily Ever After"…the fairy tales and movies have built up such a relationship paradise that I don't think any one couple could ever live up to it. I'm sure society will continue to try over and over again until we get it right or we just get tired and give up. I just might be *happy* with "Contentment Ever After." How's that for a new modern day fairy tale ending? Realistic and hopeful, yet attainable. I think I'll copyright that and try to sell it to Hallmark, make a million, and live *happily ever after*.

69

HAPPY ENDING!

Maybe there is a happy ending or a happily ever after for people like me, I would hope that there is someone out there crazier than I am. Someone who is willing to put up with my bullshit insecurities and relationship phobias to fall in love with me and keep me from running away from him. Someone who is stronger than I am and definitely much more patient…he'd have to be to actually get me and keep me in a relationship before I ruin it by just being me.

I'm the average girl just trying to find my way in the world of love, life, and livelihood. I haven't done all that well so far but at least I'm trying, definitely still trying and I don't plan on giving up any time soon. Perseverance wins out and if I'm the last girl standing, and if I'm standing alone, then I guess it means I've failed…kind of…but if I'm the last girl standing with a guy then I've won right? Whatever. At least I'm still out there after all of the tragedy in my dating life. You've got to give me a little credit for that!

I don't know if I ever will get married. It may not be in the cards for me, but that might just be because I haven't met the right guy yet. You know the one, the man of my "dreams" who will sweep me off my feet and keep me in check and stop me from being completely nuts. I'm sure if that ever happens I'll turn into one of those annoying women—in love and happy. Accidentally rubbing it in the noses of everyone I meet, making bitter chicks like me even more bitter because they haven't found their soul mates or puzzle pieces yet.

I don't doubt I'll meet mine, probably because I know I will not settle. I'd rather be alone with a bunch of cats than growing old with a man I can't stand to look at anymore or listening to him eat with his mouth open. That would drive me nuts. Being alone and easy with bad taste is a more fun than waking up next to a man that I have nothing in common with, just because I was afraid to be alone.

Whatever you do, don't give up just to be with a man or to be taken care of or to drive a nice car and live in the suburbs. Your soul mate is out there, so is your puzzle piece. I sincerely believe it's out there for you and me. You just have to be patient. I am. I'll be single until I find my one and only. Someone who I miss even when we're only apart for a couple of hours. Someone who will be my best friend and lover for all time. Someone who will care for me no matter what. He'll have faith and believe in me. He will help me; I will help him. He's out there...I KNOW HE IS!!! But until I find him, I'll just keep trolling this town for men with amazing sex drives, looking for a hot momma to keep them warm at night. I'll be here...happy, horny, and looking for action because like always, I'm easy...and I have bad taste!